845872

The Architecture of Scotland

1 Culross Palace,
Fife

The Architecture of Scotland

John G. Dunbar

B.T. Batsford Ltd, London

Copyright John G. Dunbar 1966
First published 1966
Second (revised) edition 1978
Filmset by Keyspools Ltd, Golborne, Lancs
Printed in Great Britain by
The Anchor Press Ltd, Tiptree, Essex
for the publishers B.T. Batsford Ltd,
4 Fitzhardinge Street, London W1H OAH

ISBN 0 7134 1142 2

Contents

Acknowledgements

In preparing this revised edition I have again received much help from friends and colleagues, and in particular from Mr David Walker, Miss Catherine Cruft and Mr Richard Emerson. I am also grateful to Mr Samuel Carr of B. T. Batsford Ltd for his continued advice and to my wife for her constant support and encouragement.

The Author and Publishers would like to thank the following for permission to reproduce the illustrations appearing in this book: Robert M. Adam, no. 18; Aerofilms Ltd, no. 80; G. Douglas Bolton, no. 64; J. Allan Cash, no. 28; Noel Habgood, no. 1; A.F. Kersting, nos 14, 56; Donald B. MacCulloch, no. 4; Mrs Isa MacLaren, no. 79; Ministry of Public Building and Works, Edinburgh (Crown Copyright), nos 6, 7, 10, 23, 24, 26, 41, 42, 43; Sir David Montgomery, Bart., no. 49; J. Peterson, no. 118; Geoffrey B. Quick, nos 5, 37, 66, 72, 78, 83; Royal Commission on Ancient Monuments, Scotland, nos 3, 12, 15, 17, 20, 21, 32, 33, 35, 39, 45, 46, 49, 51, 52, 53, 57, 58, 63, 69, 71, 81, 82, 84–95, 97, 98, 100, 101, 104, 106, 108, 112, 119, 120, 121; Dr J.K. St Joseph, no. 22; Scottish National Buildings Record, nos 48, 70, 73, 77, 79, 107 (Erskine Beveridge Collection), 113; Scottish Record Office, no. 54; Scottish Tourist Board, no. 62; Kenneth Scowen, no. 60; W. Suschitzky, nos 11, 31; Will F. Taylor, no. 8; Valentine & Sons, nos 30, 40; Reece Winstone, no. 59.

The line illustrations were drawn for the book by Ian G. Scott, except for nos 2, 96, 99, 102 and 103, which were done by Chartwell Illustrators. For permission to base drawings on copyright material the Publishers wish to thank the following: The Society of Antiquaries of Scotland, nos 27, 110; Ernest Benn Ltd, no. 111, from *Norse Building in the Scottish Isles*; The Clarendon Press, Oxford, and G. Hay, no. 55, from *The Architecture of Scottish Post-Reformation Churches, 1560–1843*; Country Life Ltd, no. 67, and no. 103, from *The Work of Sir Robert Lorimer*, by C. Hussey; The Trustees of George Heriot's Trust, Edinburgh, no. 44; the Publishers of R. Kerr's *The Gentleman's House*, no. 96; Oxford University Press, no. 2, from *Early Architecture of North Britain*, by C. Thomas; Royal Commission on Ancient Monuments, Scotland, nos 29, 47, 61, 76, 117.

List of Illustrations

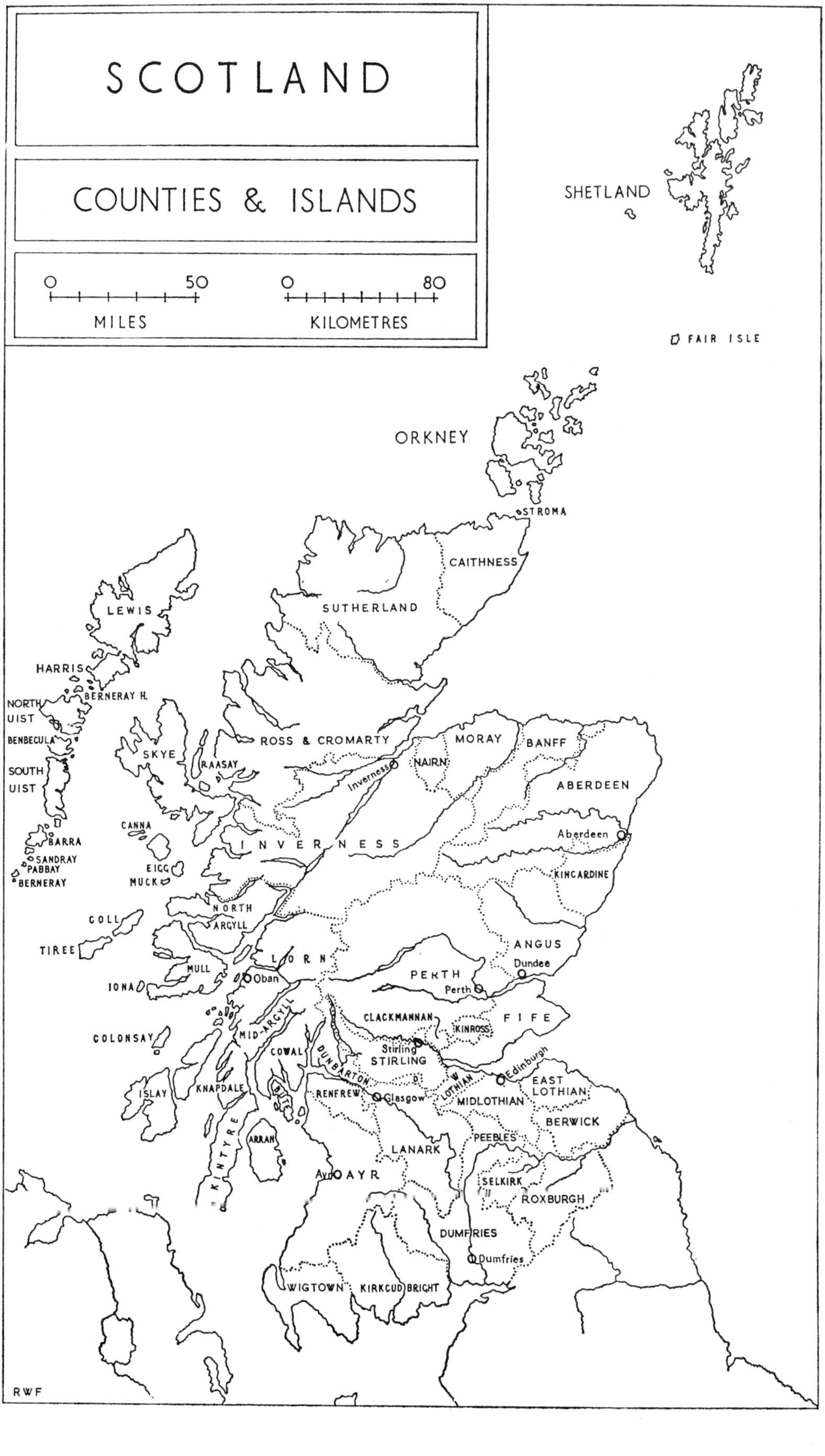

SCOTLAND

COUNTIES & ISLANDS

MILES 0 — 50

KILOMETRES 0 — 80

SHETLAND

FAIR ISLE

ORKNEY

STROMA

CAITHNESS

SUTHERLAND

LEWIS

HARRIS

BERNERAY H.

NORTH UIST

BENBECULA

SOUTH UIST

ROSS & CROMARTY

MORAY

BANFF

SKYE

RAASAY

NAIRN

Inverness

ABERDEEN

CANNA

BARRA

SANDRAY

PABBAY

BERNERAY

EIGG

MUCK

INVERNESS

Aberdeen

KINCARDINE

COLL

TIREE

NORTH ARGYLL

ANGUS

MULL

IONA

LORN

Oban

Dundee

PERTH

Perth

FIFE

COLONSAY

MID-ARGYLL

CLACKMANNAN

KINROSS

COWAL

DUNBARTON

Stirling

STIRLING

LOTHIAN

Edinburgh

EAST LOTHIAN

ISLAY

KNAPDALE

RENFREW

Glasgow

MIDLOTHIAN

BERWICK

ARRAN

PEEBLES

KINTYRE

LANARK

Ayr

AYR

SELKIRK

ROXBURGH

DUMFRIES

Dumfries

WIGTOWN

KIRKCUDBRIGHT

R W F

I

Pre-Reformation Churches

Early Churches and Monasteries

It is likely that Christianity was first introduced into Scotland on a considerable scale in about the second half of the fifth century. From early religious centres such as Carlisle and Whithorn the faith spread slowly northwards to Strathclyde and the Forth valley, its further advance into Pictland and Dalriada gaining impetus from the Irish missionary movement of the later sixth and seventh centuries, which led to the foundation of numerous monasteries, the most celebrated of these being instituted at Iona by Columba himself in 565. Although the earliest Christian missions seem to have resulted in the establishment of some kind of diocesan system in southern Scotland, the Columban movement was organised upon a monastic basis, and it was only in the eighth century that the Scottish church again began to move towards a territorial diocesan system, most of the earlier monasteries falling victim to Norse raids or being reconstituted as communities of secular clergy, often named Culdees.

At more than a millenium's remove early Christian society stands most vividly revealed in its religious literature and in the art of its sculptured stones, metalwork and illuminated manuscripts. Architectural remains are scanty and can seldom be closely dated, but literary sources and archaeological evidence alike suggest that in most parts of Scotland stone buildings were few and far between and that the materials most commonly employed in the construction of churches were timber, wattle, clay and turf. Archaeological excavation has demonstrated that in some cases an original timber church was afterwards replaced by a stone one standing on the same site. At Ardwall Isle, Kirkcudbrightshire, for example, recent excavation brought to light traces of a tiny timber oratory (11ft. by 7ft. 6ins.) of perhaps the seventh century, which had been superseded a century or so later by a somewhat larger stone-walled church. Other early stone churches in Celtic-speaking areas, such as those discovered at Whithorn itself and at St Ninian's Isle, Bute, may likewise be the eighth-century (or later) successors of timber prototypes; they are usually small single-chambered buildings of oblong plan with west doorways, all these features showing a close correspondence with Irish churches of the period.

In southern Pictland, however, the practice of building in stone appears to have been introduced from Northumbria, for it is known that in a letter

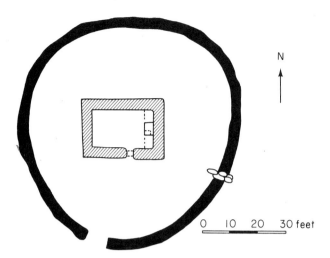

N

0   10   20   30 feet

2 Chapel, St Ninian's
Point, Bute: plan

written to the abbot of the Anglian monastery of Wearmouth in 710
Nechtan MacDerile, king of the Picts, requested that 'architects should be
sent to him to make a church of stone . . . after the manner of the Romans'.
The site of the church is not named, but it has been conjectured to have been
at Restenneth, the locality traditionally associated with Nechtan's baptism
by St Boniface, and it is possible that the lower portion of the square tower
now embedded in the medieval Augustinian priory there may have formed
part of Nechtan's church.

The buildings of a Columban monastery comprised one or more
churches, together with a number of small huts for the monks, while larger
establishments might also contain a guest-house, a refectory and perhaps a
school. In most cases the monastery was enclosed by a ditch and bank or
stone-built rampart (the *vallum monasterii*) intended to serve more as a
spiritual boundary than as a defensive barrier. At Iona the roughly oblong
enclosure seems to have measured about 1200ft. by 900ft., while the *vallum*
comprised an earthen bank with a broad outer ditch, some portions of
which are still well preserved. The earliest buildings of which traces have
been revealed by excavation were huts of turf and wattle, while standing
structures include a stone church of about the tenth century and several fine
crosses of the pre-Norse period. Similar ditched embankments can be seen
in south-east Scotland at St Abb's Head, Coldingham, and Old Melrose,
where in each case the monastery occupied a promontory site, the *vallum*
extending only across the neck of approach.

Many of the smaller monasteries of Irish type, particularly those situated
along the western and northern seaboards, were located in lonely and
almost inaccessible places, their deliberate isolation reflecting the austere
and eremitical lives of their founders in the 'Age of the Saints'. In such
places, where the ground was frequently hard and stony, it was often found
more convenient to enclose the monastery with a stout drystone wall or
cashel (Irish, *caisel*). A *vallum* of this type is preserved at Eileach an

3 Iona Nunnery, Argyll

Naoimh, in the Firth of Lorn, where St Brendan of Clonfert, the sailor-monk, established a monastery in 542. The existing remains also include a well-constructed double 'beehive' hut and two churches, the earlier of which may be as old as the 10th century; the walls are of flagstone bedded in clay mortar and the doorway has inclined jambs. The beehive hut, too, with its roofs of corbelled stone built without mortar, may well belong to the early Christian period, although in parts of western Scotland, as in Ireland, structures of this kind continued to be erected until comparatively recent times. Other probable monastic cashels occur at Ceann a' Mhara, Tiree; Nave Island, Islay; and at the somewhat enigmatic site on Canna known as Sgor nam Ban-naomha ('Cliff of the holy women'), which incorporates not only a possible beehive hut but also a remarkably sophisticated water-supply system serving both a horizontal mill and a latrine. Further north recent fieldwork has revealed an interesting series of what may have been small eremitical monasteries of Irish type perched along the cliff coasts of Orkney and Shetland, where there are also a number of similar sites, such as Strandibrough, Fetlar, and Brough of Deerness, Orkney, characterized by buildings of Norse form, which possibly belong to the twelfth and thirteenth centuries.

The most impressive surviving buildings of the early Christian period, however, are the round towers at Brechin and Abernethy which, architecturally speaking, are clearly outposts of a well-known group of Irish

4 Beehive hut, Eileach an
Naoimh, Argyll

towers of the tenth to the twelfth centuries. Designed both as belfries and
as places of security in time of war, these towers were strongly constructed
of stone and lime, the numerous floors (Brechin had seven) usually being of
timber. Brechin and Abernethy were both early episcopal centres and are
known to have been occupied by Culdee communities during the period in
which the towers were erected.

Abbeys and Priories

With the reorganisation of the Scottish church by the rulers of the Canmore
dynasty new monastic foundations, colonised initially from England and
the Continent, followed each other in rapid succession. David I (1124–53)
himself founded some dozen abbeys and priories, among which the
Cistercian and Augustinian Orders were particularly well represented. By
the end of the thirteenth century the great majority of Scotland's medieval
religious houses were already in being, most of them being situated in the
fertile southern and eastern counties. A few more houses continued to be
founded in the later Middle Ages, while others became defunct, the total
number of monastic establishments on the eve of the Reformation being
rather more than 100.

In contrast to the informal layout of the early Christian monastery, the
buildings of the new medieval foundations were erected upon a regular

plan, whose main features had become standardised on the Continent during Carolingian times, and which had been further developed and refined in the great reformed houses of Burgundy and Normandy. Such standardisation was appropriate to the more highly organised structure of the medieval religious Orders, in which the individual monastery was as closely bound to other houses of the same Order as was the individual monk to the community of which he was a member. The most distinctive feature of this plan was the cloister, a quadrangular enclosure round which there were grouped the living quarters and administrative buildings of the monks,

5 Brechin Round Tower
and Cathedral, Angus

as well as the church whose choir and altars were the focus of their daily life. Outside this claustral nucleus there stood the various offices, together with certain other structures for which a degree of seclusion was required such as the infirmary, the abbot's or prior's lodgings and, in some cases, a guest-house.

Architecturally the greater Scottish abbeys, at least, bore full comparison with their sister houses in England and the Continent, and in a country possessing few notable cathedrals or large parish churches their construction provided a rare opportunity for the display of a wide range of the visual arts. It is doubly unfortunate, therefore, that so little now remains of their carved decoration in wood and stone, of their mural paintings, coloured tiles and rich furnishings, and that the buildings within which these treasures were housed are for the most part mutilated and incomplete. Partly through neglect and mismanagement, partly through the ill chance that placed so many of the wealthier monasteries in the direct path of

6 Nave arcade,
Dunfermline Abbey, Fife

invading English armies, and partly through deliberate suppression in the days 'when ruine bare rule, and Knox knock'd downe churches', the noblest and most sumptuously furnished buildings in the country were successively destroyed or abandoned, as little regret being shown at their passing as at that of the religious communities whose dwelling-places they had been for up to four centuries.

One of the first Anglo-Norman foundations was Dunfermline, where a small Benedictine community appears to have been established by Queen Margaret in about 1070. The monastery was raised to abbatial status by David I, who brought Geoffrey, prior of Canterbury, to be first abbot there in 1128. A new church, replacing an earlier one of very modest dimensions, was probably begun about the same time, and work was sufficiently advanced to allow part at least of the building to be dedicated in 1150. Of this great cruciform structure little now remains but the nave, and even this has been shorn of its eastern bay. Nevertheless, the surviving portion ranks as one of the finest Romanesque interiors in Scotland, and the massive cylindrical piers with chevron ornament, the octagonal scalloped capitals and the triple arch-mouldings all go to suggest that the lower storey at least was the work of master-masons familiar with the bay-design of Durham Cathedral. Among the smaller Benedictine houses one of the most interesting is Coldingham, a twelfth-century foundation which succeeded the earlier monastery on St Abb's Head. The long aisleless choir of about 1200 is a remarkable composition, the two-storeyed division of the elevations and the free use of arcading accentuating the horizontal character of the design.

The reformed Benedictines of Tiron were well represented in Scotland and two of their larger houses, Kelso and Arbroath, made notable contributions to the country's architecture. Kelso, one of the wealthiest and most influential of all Scottish abbeys, was colonized directly from the mother house of Tiron, the great monastic church being founded near the royal castle and burgh of Roxburgh in 1128, following an abortive attempt to establish the monastery at Selkirk. The design is unusual inasmuch as the church incorporates transepts at both ends, a plan probably derived from the Carolingian and Romanesque churches of the Rhineland. It was from Kelso that a community was sent to Arbroath when the abbey of St Thomas Becket was founded by William the Lion in 1178. The church is of regular plan, the most interesting portions to have survived being the south transept and the west front. The former is notable for the boldness and simplicity of its window composition, while the latter incorporates, between heavily-buttressed towers of massive proportions, a remarkable centrepiece in which the west doorway is recessed beneath an arcaded gallery. This gallery was intended for liturgical use, as for example when the west doors were opened for processional purposes, and similar structures formerly existed at St Andrews Cathedral and at Holyrood Abbey.

The third main branch of the Benedictine family, the Order of Cluny,

7 Kelso Abbey,
Roxburghshire

had only two Scottish houses, Paisley and Crossraguel. The abbey church of
Paisley is for the most part of late medieval date, but the general design and
proportions of the nave evidently follow those of a thirteenth-century
building of which certain fragments remain, notably an elaborate west
doorway. The bay-design of the nave incorporates a curious clerestory-
gallery which, instead of being wholly contained within the wall-thickness,
is carried round the main piers on projecting corbels – a rather clumsy
variation of a structural expedient that may be seen employed to better
effect at Rouen Cathedral. At Crossraguel the long narrow aisleless church
of the early fifteenth century terminates in a three-sided apse, a type of ending
more usually associated with collegiate churches. The abbot's lodgings
were evidently grouped round a triangular courtyard situated beyond the
east range of the cloister. Their most conspicuous feature is a sixteenth-
century tower-house of uncompromisingly secular aspect, presumably the

residence either of one of the latter-day abbots or of a lay commendator holding a grant of the monastic revenues.

The close intercourse that existed between the court of David I and the leaders of the Cistercian movement in England ensured the rapid establishment of the White Monks in the northern kingdom. In 1136, only seven years after the foundation of the first English community of the Order, a colony was sent north from Rievaulx to establish a monastery at Melrose, in its turn to become the parent of no less than five of the eleven Cistercian houses instituted by the end of the fifteenth century. Little now remains of the small plain church that served the early needs of the community – a generation whose ears were still ringing with St Bernard's eloquent denunciations of all forms of architectural embellishment. By the time the abbey came to be rebuilt at the end of the fourteenth century this attitude had been abandoned and the new church was conceived upon much more ambitious lines. The plan itself was an enlarged version of the original one, the east end retaining its echelon form and the south aisle being provided with an additional series of chapels. A complete scheme of rib-vaulting was envisaged (a rare occurrence in Scotland) and the sculptured decoration was to be of the highest quality. The project was unfinished when work stopped in the early sixteenth century, but even so the

8 Melrose Abbey, Roxburghshire

completed portion ranks as one of the most accomplished examples of late medieval ecclesiastical architecture in the country. On stylistic grounds the design can be attributed to master-masons of the northern English school, the east arm in particular bearing the stamp of the York masons' yard. The curvilinear tracery of the great south transept-window, on the other hand, suggests influences from northern France and may probably be ascribed to John Morow, a master-mason of French extraction ('born in Parysse certainly'), whose career is set out in a contemporary mural inscription.

Two other houses of the Order are of special interest, Dundrennan, because it illustrates the early Cistercian Gothic style that was developed in northern Britain during the second half of the twelfth century, and New Abbey, because its church is more complete than that of any other Cistercian monastery. The plans of these two Kirkcudbrightshire houses were very much alike, each church having a west porch, aisled nave, transepts with eastern chapels, and a square-ended presbytery. The spacious and dignified design of the Dundrennan crossing and transepts, as

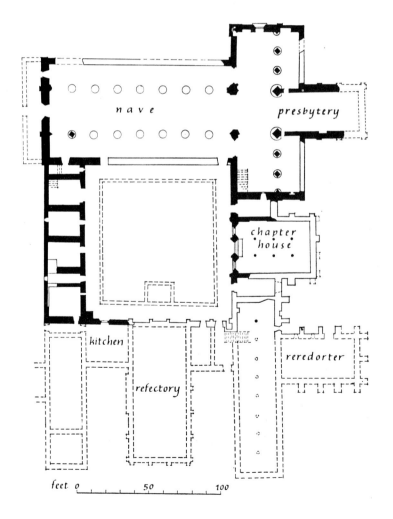

9 Dundrennan Abbey, Kircudbrightshire: plan

feet 0   50   100

remodelled in the late twelfth century to incorporate an additional third storey, reflects the influence of contemporary work in some Yorkshire houses of the Order, such as Roche and Byland. Although well preserved, the fourteenth-century church of New Abbey is architecturally un-distinguished, much of its detail, such as the geometric window-tracery of the presbytery, being heavy and uninspired.

Closely allied to the Cistercian Order was that of Vallis Caulium, which had three Scottish houses, all founded within a year or two of one another. The most important architecturally is Pluscardine, established as a Valliscaulian house by Alexander II in 1230, but transferred to the Benedictine Order in the fifteenth century. The plan of the church evidently dates from the original foundation, the aisleless choir being square-ended and each transept having two eastern chapels. Beauly has a simple cruciform plan and the long unaisled nave and short transepts recall the form of the first English Cistercian churches, erected a hundred years earlier. The third member of the trio, Ardchattan, is closer to Pluscardine in plan, although the transeptal chapels are unusually shallow and the nave includes a narrow north aisle. The fifteenth-century monastic refectory, now incorporated within a later mansion, still preserves its arcaded pulpit and open timber roof.

The Augustinians were among the most popular of the religious Orders in medieval Scotland, having two nunneries and 18 houses of canons, of which one was the monastic cathedral of St Andrews. The smaller foundations have left few traces, although two west highland houses, Oransay Priory and Iona Nunnery, have remains of some curiosity and interest, the latter retaining a remarkable early thirteenth-century church which shows the same mingling of Irish and mainland Scottish Transitional styles that is apparent in the adjacent Benedictine abbey. The larger and more generously endowed Augustinian monasteries, however, form a notable group, Holyrood, Jedburgh and Cambuskenneth all retaining substantial fragments of medieval buildings.

The quality of the original design of Holyrood must now be judged primarily from the early thirteenth-century west front, which stands out as one of the most harmonious compositions of its kind. Above the elaborate west doorway and its tribune gallery the two great west windows originally rose to the nave vault, while tiers of sculptured arcading bound this central unit to square flanking-towers capped by spires. At Jedburgh, another of David I's foundations, a good deal of mid-twelfth-century work remains in the crossing and choir, where the triforia are included within the main pier-arcades, a device intended to give an appearance of height to what would otherwise be a relatively low interior. Cambuskenneth is now represented mainly by a fine detached belfry of late thirteenth-century date, while the island monastery of Inchcolm is of interest on account of its well-preserved claustral buildings. These belong largely to the fourteenth century, but the east range incorporates an earlier chapter-house of polygonal plan. The

10 Jedburgh Abbey, Roxburghshire

most unusual feature of the design is the cloister walk, which is wholly contained within the ground-floor area of the surrounding claustral buildings, an arrangement found also in a number of late medieval Irish religious houses.

The Premonstratensians had only six Scottish communities, and one of these served the monastic cathedral of the bishops of Whithorn. Apart from Whithorn Cathedral itself, the only surviving remains of importance are those of Dryburgh, which was founded by Hugh de Moreville in 1150 and ranked as the first house of the Order in Scotland. The church comprised an aisled nave, short transepts with eastern chapels, and a square-ended presbytery having side chapels in echelon. The elevational design of the crossing and transepts offers another solution to the problem of incorporating a conventional three-storeyed system of pier-arcade, triforium and clerestory within a building of modest height, but whereas the triforium of the Jedburgh choir is encompassed within the main arcade, the Dryburgh triforium retains separate identity through compression into a series of small quatrefoil openings set one in each bay.

Cathedrals

David I's reorganisation of bishops' sees left the kingdom with ten dioceses, and an eleventh was created in the 1180s, at which time Argyll was separated from Dunkeld. Three other sees remained nominally outside the Scottish province until the erection of the bishopric of St Andrews into an archbishopric in 1472, when Galloway was transferred from the province of York, and Orkney and the Isles from Trondheim. The administrative changes of the twelfth century inevitably gave rise to considerable architectural activity, which culminated in a notable period of cathedral building during the following century.

Few churches of undisputed cathedral status antedate the diocesan reorganisation of the twelfth century. The tall primitive-looking tower of Dunblane Cathedral may in part be as old as the late eleventh century, however, while early buildings also survive in the dioceses of St Andrews and perhaps also Orkney, where new cathedrals were subsequently erected upon different sites. Although small, the church on the Brough of Birsay is a structure of considerable interest, the plan comprising a western tower, aisleless nave and apsidal choir. This is now generally identified as the 'splendid minster' of Christchurch that Earl Thorfinn erected following his return from pilgrimage in about 1050, and which became the cathedral of Orkney early in the following century, but there is evidence to support the traditional view which places the site of Christchurch in the vicinity of the present parish church of Birsay.

Like Birsay, St Rule's Church, St Andrews, is of markedly individualistic character. Of narrow proportions and massive construction, its towering walls pierced by small double-splayed windows set high above ground, the choir at once recalls Northumbrian building practice of pre-Conquest times. The tall square tower with round-headed two-light windows also belongs to the late Anglo-Saxon or early Anglo-Norman tradition, but can be paralleled elsewhere in Scotland, notably at Dunblane, Dunning and Muthill. Some of these towers, such as Dunning, appear in fact to be of late Norman date, but St Rule's itself is now usually regarded as belonging to the time of Queen Margaret (1070–93).

Birsay retained its episcopal status for no more than a generation, for in 1137 Earl Rognvald founded a new cathedral at Kirkwall, dedicating it to his murdered kinsman St Magnus. Orkney's political affiliations were with the Norse world, but the Earl and his father, Kol, who is said to have supervised the building of the cathedral, were no doubt aware of contemporary architectural developments in western Europe. It was probably as a direct result of their initiative that the influence of the Durham school, already apparent in the design of Dunfermline Abbey, now penetrated to Orkney. As first laid out the cathedral of St Magnus appears to have comprised an aisled nave of eight bays with western towers, transepts with eastern apsidioles, and an aisled choir of three bays terminating in a central apse. Although the original scheme was subsequently modified during construction, the building retains a strong underlying unity, while the excellence of the proportions effectively disguises its smallness of size. As it stands today the oldest portions of the cathedral are the transepts and the adjacent bays of the nave and choir, which seem to have been completed about the middle of the twelfth

11 St Rule's Church, St Andrews, Fife

century; the bay-design is tripartite, the cylindrical piers of the main arcades being much more massive than those of Dunfermline.

At St Andrews, too, plans for a new cathedral were being made by Bishop Robert, who had brought a community of Augustinian canons to the church of St Rule's in about 1127. The building whose walls began to rise on an adjacent site in 1160, a year after Bishop Robert's death, was conceived on a noble scale, its nave of 14 bays making it one of the longest churches in

12 Kirkwall Cathedral, Orkney

Britain. Unfortunately, little now survives apart from the east gable, which originally incorporated three tiers of triplet windows, and the loss of the remainder is one of the tragedies of Scottish architectural history. Surrounding the cathedral there is a well-preserved precinct wall fortified with round and rectangular towers, and having a stately entrance-gateway on its west side.

Among the cathedrals that took shape during the intensive building activity of the thirteenth century, the most important are Glasgow, Dunblane and Elgin. The site upon which Bishop Bondington of Glasgow began to raise his new cathedral soon after 1233 had been sacred since early

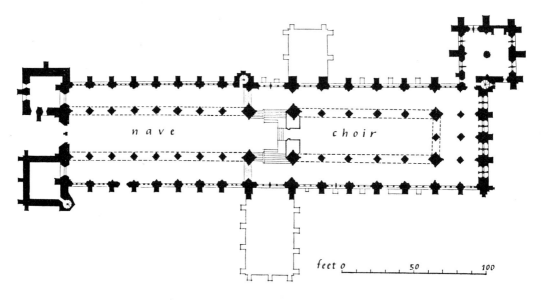

nave

choir

feet 0   50   100

13 Glasgow Cathedral: plan

Christian times and must already have borne a succession of churches, each in turn enshrining the relics of St Mungo. Although Bondington's cathedral incorporated only a few fragments of its immediate forerunner of the late twelfth and early thirteenth centuries, the new church did, however, retain its predecessor's distinctive two-level arrangement of the eastern arm. This gave the designer an opportunity to create a double choir of unusual dignity and splendour in which the shrine of St Mungo could stand behind the high altar in the upper church while the saint's tomb, placed directly beneath the high altar, became the focus of the lower church. The western portion of the cathedral, completed during the fourteenth century, comprises an aisled nave and high transepts of the same width as the main vessel, but the work is inferior in quality to that seen in the eastern arm. Early in the fifteenth century the canons' stalls were moved eastwards to allow the whole of the nave to be used for preaching, and the new ritual choir thus formed was screened off by a massive stone *pulpitum*, the only one of its kind now to survive in Scotland.

About the time that Bishop Bondington was beginning his work of reconstruction at Glasgow another ambitious building scheme was commenced at Dunblane, where a new church was laid out to comprise an aisled nave of eight bays and a spacious unaisled choir some 8oft. in length; no provision was made for transepts. The most successful feature of the composition is the nave, where the elegant proportions of the main arcade and galleried clerestory more than compensate for the omission of a triforium. In the diocese of Moray a start was made upon the reconstruction of an existing church at Elgin early in the thirteenth century, when the transference of the episcopal seat thither from Spynie was under active consideration. The first cathedral was a modest structure comprising an aisled nave, transepts, and a square-ended aisleless choir; there were twin western towers and a third above the crossing. The partial destruction of this building by fire in 1270 opened the way for a far-reaching scheme of enlargement in which the nave was provided with double aisles on each side – a rare occurrence in Britain – and the choir was extended eastwards to a length of seven bays and flanked by slightly shorter aisles; at the same time an octagonal chapter-house was erected on the north side of the choir. This great cathedral church, 'the ornament of the realm, the glory of the kingdom, the delight of foreigners and stranger guests', was slighted by Alexander Stewart, 'Wolf of Badenoch', in 1390 and although the damage was afterwards made good the fabric was allowed to become ruinous after the Reformation.

Although none of the buildings just described achieves the refinement of the developed Gothic style of the Ile de France, all exhibit certain general characteristics of that style such as are common to contemporary structures in other western European countries. After the end of the thirteenth century, however, Scottish architecture rapidly lost touch with developments in England and the Continent and, apart from one or two obviously derivative compositions, such as the east end of Melrose Abbey, ecclesiastical buildings of all ranks were absorbed within the vernacular tradition. Scottish church architecture of this period is characterised by a reversion to earlier forms such as the round arch and cylindrical pier, by the development of an increasingly whimsical repertoire of detail, and by the adoption of certain structural features of castellated origin of which the most conspicuous is the barrel-vault. This native ecclesiastical style of the

14 Elgin Cathedral, Morayshire

later Middle Ages cannot be said to possess great aesthetic merit, nor does it always conform to accepted principles of design, but its directness of form and frankness of expression give it an attraction of its own.

Many of these vernacular mannerisms appear in the cathedrals that were re-built during the fifteenth and early sixteenth centuries. St Machar's Aberdeen, for example, retains an aisled nave and western towers of the second quarter of the fifteenth century. The main arcades incorporate plain

15 St Machar's
Cathedral, Aberdeen

cylindrical piers having simply moulded bases and capitals. The clerestory windows, on the other hand, and the remarkable seven-light window in the west wall, are round-arched, the latter being enriched with cusped inner heads. The severity of the west front reflects the nature of the material of which it is built, every part, with the exception of the spires, being constructed of local granite; there is a complete absence of carved decoration and the mouldings of the processional doorway are rudimentary in character. The barrel-vaulted towers are defensive in aspect if not in function, the heavily buttressed walls rising to a corbelled and machicolated parapet such as might have crowned a contemporary tower-house.

The layout at Dunkeld has a good deal in common with that of the neighbouring cathedral of Dunblane, and may reflect the plan of a thirteenth-century building of which only a few fragments now remain. The extensive unaisled choir was almost entirely reconstructed in the early nineteenth century, but the aisled nave of seven bays and the north-west tower are of fifteenth-century date, the cylindrical columns and pointed arches of the main arcades being similar to those at St Machar's. The triforium openings are semicircular and have pointed inner arches with trefoiled heads, while the clerestory comprises a series of small pointed windows of the plainest description. An attempt to improve the design of the west front by the insertion of a new entrance and great window has produced a curiously unbalanced composition in which the ogee canopy of the inserted window tries to jostle an earlier gable-light out of position.

Churches

In Scotland, as in England, local ecclesiastical districts, or *parochia*, seem at first to have been centred upon churches of minster type staffed by resident bodies of priests serving fairly wide areas. During the twelfth century, however, a predominantly feudal pattern of parochial organisation began to emerge in southern and eastern Scotland as landowners, many of them of Anglo-Norman origin, built and endowed churches in their own localities. Indeed, in some areas the boundaries of barony and parish were frequently coterminous, the church itself often being placed close to the baronial residence, as at Leuchars where the Romanesque church stands only a few hundred yards from the motte-and-bailey castle of the de Quinceys.

In the more feudalized parts of the country, at least, Scottish churches of the twelfth and thirteenth centuries showed a fairly close correspondence with their counterparts in England. But whereas the majority of English parish churches were enlarged or rebuilt during the later Middle Ages, almost each generation leaving its mark on the fabric, there was comparatively little church building in Scotland at this period except in the burghs and in certain rural areas of central Scotland where lay magnates established collegiate foundations. The average Scottish parish church remained small in size and relatively unadorned, and it was only after a further two centuries or so of post-Reformation neglect that a new generation of improving lairds undertook an extensive programme of rebuilding, which swept away the majority of medieval buildings and dotted the landscape with the trim Georgian kirks that are seen today. The general architectural inferiority of the later medieval parish church was also no doubt due partly to the fact that in some areas of the country the pattern of settlement was so scattered that spiritual needs could most effectively be met by the erection of a number of small dependent chapels rather than one sizeable church, and partly to the fact that a very high proportion of Scottish parish churches became appropriated to religious houses, a considerable portion of the parochial revenues thus being diverted from local use.

The typical Romanesque parish church of the eastern lowlands comprised an oblong nave and small square-ended chancel; the timber roof was covered with thatch or shingles and the deeply-splayed windows admitted a bare minimum of light. There was little ornament and the furnishings were of the plainest, while the internal wall-surfaces were usually limewashed, perhaps bearing a simple pattern of painted decoration. Although a considerable number of such churches was built, the majority of surviving examples are now fragmentary, but Duddingston and Aberdour retain their Romanesque identities, while the little hilltop kirk of

16 Birnie Church, Morayshire: plan

Birnie survives almost intact, its narrow chancel-arch of two plain orders springing from heavy scalloped capitals of conventional Norman pattern. In a few places, such as Rutherglen, churches of more elaborate type were erected for parochial use, but only at St Nicholas's Aberdeen, is there any evidence of the existence of a fully developed aisled and cruciform building of Romanesque date. Dalmeny has a western tower, an oblong nave and a square choir with an apse, both choir and apse being vaulted. The whole fabric is executed in ashlar masonry and there is a fine display of carved detail. Other closely related examples of the same type survive in more fragmentary condition at Tynninghame and Leuchars, where the external walls of the choir and apse are enriched with two tiers of arcading. Unique in Scotland among churches of this period is the circular nave at Orphir in Orkney, one of a number of round churches erected in western Europe during the time of the Crusades after the model of the Church of the Holy Sepulchre at Jerusalem.

The typical post-Romanesque parish church was an aisleless building of elongated unicameral plan, the chancel being separated from the nave simply by a timber screen. Good examples of thirteenth-century churches of this type occur at Abdie and Auchindoir, while the well-preserved remains

17 Dalmeny Church,
West Lothian, after R.W.
Billings

of the old parish kirk of Cawdor at Barevan are of special interest because the character of the architectural detail associates the building with the near-by hall-house of Rait (p. 47). The church measures about 70ft. in length, the nave and chancel being more or less equal in size; the chancel was lit by a series of simple lancet-windows. Structures of this type went on being built right up to the Reformation and beyond, and the plan and dimensions of Barevan can be paralleled in later medieval churches such as Kinkell, whose sixteenth-century character becomes apparent only when account is taken of its carved detail.

Nearly all the larger Scottish burghs must have been provided with their own parish churches from the earliest times, but with the exception of some fragments at Aberdeen no major burgh kirks of twelfth- or thirteenth-century date now survive. Sometimes, as at Linlithgow and Stirling, these earlier churches were destroyed by accident or assault, but more frequently they were pulled down because of decay or because their accommodation had become inadequate, for during the fifteenth and sixteenth centuries an improvement in the economic position of a number of the more important towns provided an opportunity for fresh building projects to be undertaken.

Burghs vied with one another in the erection of costly new edifices, whose numerous chapels and altars bore witness to the piety and prosperity of the merchants and craftsmen who endowed them.

Some of these churches bear a strong family resemblance to each other and most are comparable in size to the smaller Scottish cathedrals, being designed as aisled cruciform buildings with one or more towers. The reconstruction of the parish church of St Giles', Edinburgh, began in the late

18 Holy Rude Church, Stirling

fourteenth century, the new building comprising a vaulted nave of five bays flanked by double aisles, a crossing tower, short transepts and an aisled choir of four bays. Further additions continued to be made up to the second decade of the sixteenth century, and much interesting carved detail of the period survived a somewhat insensitive restoration in 1829. Second only to St Giles' among the burgh kirks of the Lothians was St Mary's, Haddington, which was completed about the middle of the fifteenth century and whose choir and crossing have recently been restored to bring the entire structure back into ecclesiastical use for the first time since the Reformation. Some of the detail, including the fine round-arched west doorway, recalls work at St Giles', while the tower is known originally to have been crowned with an open-work spire similar to those at St Giles' and at King's College, Aberdeen.

In central and eastern Scotland there may be seen some fragments of the old burgh kirks of Dundee and Aberdeen, the interesting but over-restored remains of St John's, Perth, and two well-preserved major churches of some

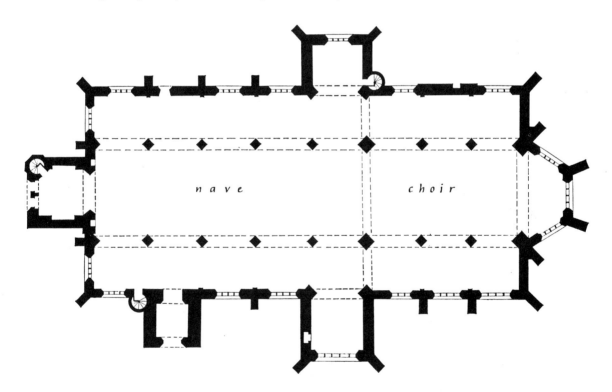

nave   choir

importance, Holy Rude, Stirling, and St Michael's Linlithgow. Both these churches replaced earlier buildings destroyed by fire in the early fifteenth century and both took a century or more to complete. A similar design was adopted in each case, the plan comprising a west tower, an aisled nave and choir of five and three bays respectively, transepts, and an apsidal presbytery of polygonal form. At Stirling it was intended to erect a second

19 Linlithgow Church, West Lothian: plan

tower above the crossing, but the project was abandoned before the supporting piers had been carried to their full height.

During the later Middle Ages the munificent piety of the Scottish baronial class found its chief expression not, as previously, in the foundation of monasteries and parish churches, but in the endowment of non-monastic communities of secular clergy known as collegiate churches. Many of these colleges were new foundations having no parochial commitments, while others were established within existing parish churches both burghal and rural, and within universities. Whether a church was newly founded or simply raised in status some form of building activity was likely to result, priority usually being given to the erection of a choir and chancel so that divine office could commence. In many cases, however, the endowments appear to have been insufficient to permit the construction of a nave, and churches were left unfinished.

One or two of the smaller collegiate churches such as Innerpeffray and Fowlis Easter followed the standard oblong form of the simpler parish kirks. Fowlis Easter itself, founded by a local laird about the year 1453, is a particularly well-preserved example; it retains part of its original timber rood-screen, an elaborate sacrament-house and some notable painted decoration. More typically, however, collegiate churches were of cruciform

20 Corstorphine
Collegiate Church,
Edinburgh

21 King's College
Chapel, Aberdeen.
Carved stalls

plan, having well-defined choirs with square or polygonal east ends; choir
and transepts were unaisled, being ceiled with heavily buttressed barrel-
vaults whose low springing-level restricted the height of the window
openings. Many of the surviving churches of this type are in the Lothians,
where polygonal-ended choirs can be seen at Dalkeith and Seton and
square-ended ones at Corstorphine, Crichton and Dunglass; only at this
last does a pre-Reformation nave remain intact. The most ambitious of all
Scottish collegiate churches was Roslin, which was founded by William St

Clair, Earl of Orkney, in 1446. This was intended to be a fully-developed cruciform structure, but only the choir was completed, together with an adjacent sacristy which extends eastwards at a lower level. The aisled choir is of five bays, the aisles returning across the east end to form an ambulatory beyond which there is a series of chapels. This plan may have been modelled upon that of Glasgow Cathedral, but there are also indications of borrowings from other and perhaps more distant sources in the curious transverse barrel-vaults of the side-aisles and the rich Plateresque decoration. Finally mention may be made of the chapel of King's College, Aberdeen, which is unique among Scottish medieval churches in possessing its original carved screen and stalls as well as a fine oak ceiling.

2
Castles and Tower-Houses

Motte-and-Bailey Castles

The earliest Scottish castles were built in the twelfth century by immigrant Anglo-Norman barons to secure lands granted to them by King David I and his successors. They bore a close resemblance to their counterparts in England and France and like them served not only as private strongholds but also as outposts of royal authority and centres of local administration and justice.

These castles were constructed mainly of earth and timber and by reason of the temporary nature of the materials used only scanty traces of them can be seen today. Moreover, the surviving remains can be misleading unless interpreted in the light of contemporary documentary and pictorial evidence, as well as of that more recently obtained by excavation. But when all these sources are drawn upon a fairly clear picture of the typical motte-and-bailey castle begins to emerge. The earthworks comprised a small circular mound (French *motte*) standing within, or adjacent to, a larger enclosure (the bailey) whose limits were defined by a ditch and cast-up bank. Upon the top of the motte, and within a strong encircling palisade, there stood a wooden tower, the citadel that formed the last refuge of the defenders. Sometimes, however, there was no separate motte, but only a massively embanked enclosure of circular or oval plan, castles of this type often being known as 'ringworks'. Within the bailey there were grouped buildings of a more domestic nature, some providing additional accommodation and others, such as stables, kitchens and storerooms, meeting the day-to-day service requirements of the lord, his family and his followers. The bailey, too, might be protected by a palisade, and both motte and bailey had their own entrance, that of the former sometimes being reached by means of a flying bridge.

Such are the castles so vividly portrayed in the Bayeux Tapestry, and such, in its essential characteristics, appears to have been Somerled of Argyll's castle in Galloway as it is described in an early thirteenth-century romance, though in this case the tower was built not of timber but of forced earth and clay, its high battlemented walls effectively protecting it from assault. The description of the surviving remains of another Galloway castle, the Mote of Urr, may serve as a guide to the principal features that are likely to be encountered by a present-day visitor to one of these sites.

22 Mote of Urr,
Kirkcudbrightshire

Here the motte stands towards the south end of an unusually large bailey, some 5½ acres in extent, above which it rises to a height of more than 30ft., the summit having a diameter of about 85ft. The motte is separated from the bailey by a broad ditch, while the bailey itself is protected by a still wider ditch which is crossed at one point by an entrance causeway. Recent archaeological investigation has been frustrated by earlier disturbance, but excavations carried out in 1957 on the summit of a Stirlingshire motte, the Keir Knowe of Drum, brought to light traces of what was probably a small timber tower surrounded by stockades.

No complete inventory of motte-and-bailey castles has yet been made, but it is probable that at least 200 structures of this type still survive in Scotland. The distribution of known sites is significant, for they are found predominantly in the south-west, less commonly throughout other parts of southern Scotland (although not, surprisingly, in the Lothians) and in the eastern lowlands between the Forth and the Moray Firth, and hardly at all in the far north and west. They occur, that is to say, in areas where there is known to have been Anglo-Norman penetration in the twelfth and early thirteenth centuries and they are virtually absent from those regions where the authority of the Scottish Crown was not recognised until a much later period. Sometimes it is possible to associate a site with a grant of land to a particular individual, as in the case of the motte of Annan, which is probably the 'castellum' referred to in David I's charter of about 1124 granting Annandale to Robert Brus.

Such castles, easily built and readily defensible, made ideal bases for a first generation of settlers, but were hardly suitable as the permanent residences of a feudal aristocracy. Once the ascendancy of the Anglo-Norman baronage was firmly established, therefore, a number of the wealthier landowners began to erect stone castles. Nevertheless, some motte-and-bailey castles and ringworks probably remained in use long after it had become fashionable to build in stone and lime. Others, like Urquhart, were absorbed into later stone castles or, like Rothesay and Duffus, were refashioned in stone without losing their original plans.

Castles of Enclosure

The earliest stone castles in Scotland that can be identified with any degree of confidence comprised a stout curtain-wall of masonry, pierced with few openings, enclosing a courtyard round which there were ranged lean-to buildings of stone or timber. These simple castles of enclosure, as they may conveniently be called, were not unlike the contemporary 'shell-keeps' of England and Normandy. Whereas the latter usually stood upon artificial mounds and were circular in plan, however, the Scottish examples were often built upon natural outcrops of rock (which the local terrain seldom failed to provide) and were frequently polygonal or rectangular in plan. The erection of a stone wall round the summit of a hillock scarcely presented a novel solution to problems of defence in North Britain, however, and while the stone castle was no doubt a foreign import so far as its technology was concerned, its form may well have been derived from native forts and brochs of an earlier age.

Many of the existing castles of this type are to be found in the west highlands, where their chances of survival during the later Middle Ages were perhaps higher than elsewhere. The earliest of these, Castle Sween, was probably built in about the last quarter of the twelfth century by Sweyn, lord of Knapdale, a member of an important local family connected by marriage to several major Irish and Scottish kindreds. As first constructed the castle comprised a quadrangular curtain-wall measuring 84ft. by 70ft., against the inner face of which three ranges of timber buildings were disposed round a small court. The curtain has flat pilaster-buttresses at the angles and mid-points, the one in the south wall containing a semicircular-headed doorway. These features, which are clearly Romanesque in character, suggest that Sweyn's master-mason was brought from southern

Scotland or Ireland. Not long afterwards the Campbell family of Loch Awe erected a similar castle at Innis Chonnell, while others soon followed both in Argyll and further north (by the Comyns) at Castle Roy, in the valley of the upper Spey. There are also a number of simple polygonal castles of enclosure in the west highlands, for example Mingary and Tioram, which like a similar group in the north of Ireland can be ascribed to the thirteenth century.

A larger variety of the rectangular castle of enclosure, measuring about 120ft. square and perhaps accommodating four ranges of courtyard buildings, was sometimes erected by the Crown or greater barons. Thus Kincardine, in the Mearns, may date from the reign of William the Lion (1165–1214), while Tarbert and Kinclaven were probably built by Alexander II (1214–49), the former to establish strategic control over Kintyre and the Clyde basin and the latter to replace an earlier royal residence at Perth.

Castles of circular plan were less common and at Rothesay the line taken

23 Castle Tioram, Inverness-shire

by the curtain seems to follow that of an older earthwork. Recent investigations have shown that the flanking-towers are later additions and that the castle originally comprised a plain shell-wall with a simple arched entrance. The masonry of the curtain is similar to that seen in the nearby late twelfth-century church of Kilblaan and this suggests that the castle was built by Alan the Steward, who gained possession of Bute at about that time. Cubbie Roo's castle on Wyre, in Orkney, also comprises a roughly circular enclosure surrounded by a strong but roughly built wall now only a few feet high. Whether this, or the small square tower that stands inside the enclosure, was the stone castle that Kolbein Kruga, 'a man from Norway', is recorded to have built here about the middle of the twelfth century is uncertain, and the search for other surviving remains of early Scandinavian castles in Scotland has so far proved no more conclusive.

During the thirteenth century a more developed type of castle of enclosure began to appear in Scotland in response to improvements in the art of fortification made in Western Europe and the Near East. Greater emphasis was now placed upon the defence of the curtain wall, which was frequently reinforced by a plinth or apron and equipped with archers slits and battlements, projecting towers often being added to provide flanking fire and to serve as mounts for catapults. At the same time special care was taken to protect the weakest point in the curtain, namely the entrance, and the gatehouse began to evolve as a key-point in the system of defence. Outworks, such as ditches, forewalls and palisades, were also constructed with the aim of keeping the attacker sufficiently far away from the curtain to frustrate the use of short-range weapons of assault.

Most of these features are illustrated by one or other of the great Scottish castles of enclosure. The circular flanking-towers that were added to the twelfth-century curtain at Rothesay have already been mentioned, while similar towers can be seen at Tarbert, where Robert I enlarged the original castle by the construction of an extensive outer bailey. Lochindorb, on the other hand, an island stronghold of the Comyn lords of Badenoch, was designed from the first to incorporate angle-towers, which are well provided with firing-slits. No special arrangements seem to have been made for the protection of the entrance, but on one side of the castle there is an outer enclosure equipped with its own portcullis-gateway. Several of these castles were provided with a keep or donjon, although this often involved no more than making one of the towers of enceinte larger and stronger than its fellows so that it could accommodate the lord and his retinue in maximum security. Inverlochy is an excellent example of an arrangement of this kind. The plan is symmetrical and comprises a quadrangular courtyard about 100ft. square strengthened at each angle by a massive circular tower. The north-west tower is planned as a keep, its residential accommodation including latrines and at least one fireplace. Other points of interest at Inverlochy are the long narrow firing-slits and splayed base-plinths of the towers, and the concentric ditch and outer bank.

24 Bothwell Castle, Lanarkshire

The two entrances at Inverlochy are no more than simple gateways in the curtain-wall, but Bothwell and Kildrummy have both keeps and well-developed gatehouses. The ambitious scale upon which the former was conceived by its builder, Walter de Moravia, in about the third quarter of the thirteenth century is at once apparent from its plan. Here provision was made not only for an exceptionally large enclosure strengthened by angle-towers and a double-towered gatehouse, but also for a massive circular donjon so designed that it could be isolated from the remainder of the castle. Much of the enclosure was never completed, however, while the donjon was partially dismantled by its owner in about 1337 lest it should again house an English garrison. More than 30 years earlier it had withstood Edward I and his army for three weeks before yielding to assault by mine, catapult and siege-tower. The walls rise to a height of nearly 90ft., and measure about 15ft. in thickness, all the facework being composed of excellent ashlar masonry. The first-floor entrance is contained within a projecting spur approached by means of a drawbridge spanning a wet moat. Additional security was provided by a portcullis, and there was also a projecting timber gallery at the wall-head from which missiles could be directed upon assailants attempting the passage of the moat. Within the donjon the lord's private hall occupied the first floor and there were two upper floors as well as a basement equipped with its own draw-well. Kildrummy was probably designed for the Earl of Mar by one of Edward I's master-masons shortly before 1300, and some features of the building strongly recall the contemporary Edwardian castles of North Wales. The enclosure, which is slightly smaller than that of Bothwell, incorporates a circular keep, angle-towers and a gatehouse, while within the north-east angle there is a group of three buildings comprising hall, kitchens and chapel.

In some castles the gatehouse itself was designed to serve as a keep. At Caerlaverock the ground-floor of the gatehouse was occupied by guardrooms, but the upper floors appear to have been residential and there are traces of a spacious vaulted hall on the first floor. The castle has a distinctive triangular plan, likened by one contemporary to a shield, 'for it had but three sides round it, with a tower at each corner, but one of them was a double one, so high, so long and so wide that the gate was underneath it, well made and strong, with a drawbridge and a sufficiency of other defences. And it had good walls, and good ditches filled right up to the brim with water.' The plan of the mid-fourteenth-century castle of Tantallon, on the other hand, has been adapted to suit a promontory site impregnable on all sides save one, where there was constructed a massive curtain-wall having a central gatehouse and terminal towers. The gatehouse was originally square on plan and contained a well-defended entrance passage on the lower floors and residential accommodation above.

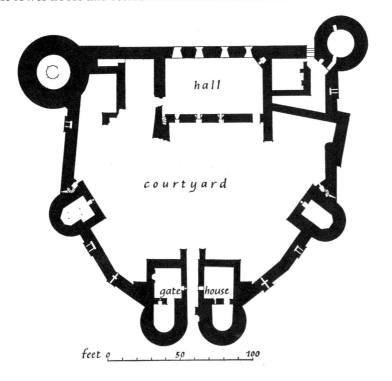

feet 0   50   100

25 Kildrummy Castle, Aberdeenshire: plan

Hall-Houses

Not all Scottish castles of the early medieval period, however, were as large or elaborate as those just described. If a baron required a residence on one of his lesser estates, or at some place where military considerations were not paramount, he sometimes found it more convenient to erect a smaller and more domestic type of building now generally known as a hall-house or fortified manor-house. These hall-houses, which smaller landowners might also build as principal residences, were compact self-contained structures of modest size usually comprising an undercroft together with a spacious first-floor hall, which often rose to an open timber roof enclosed by an open wall-walk. In some cases additional living-space was provided on an upper floor or in an adjacent wing or angle-tower, while separate service-quarters of stone or timber might be erected within an enclosing bailey. For its defence the hall-house relied mainly upon stout walls and a well-protected entrance, which was frequently situated at first-floor level.

One of the largest and most impressive surviving examples of a hall-house is Morton Castle, probably built at the turn of the thirteenth and fourteenth centuries. At one end of the main block, which measures about 100ft. in length, there is a heavily-defended gatehouse and at the other a round tower. The kitchen was in the undercroft while the hall above,

26 Rait Castle,
Nairnshire

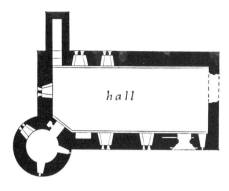

hall

27 Rait Castle,
Nairnshire: plan

perhaps the most imposing of its kind, was lit by large mullioned windows and heated by one, if not two, canopied fireplaces. Rait Castle, probably erected by Sir Gervase de Rait, soon after 1300, presents a simplified version of the same plan. There is no gatehouse, and the hall-house seems to have been freestanding within a walled and partly ditched enclosure. Again the undercroft was unvaulted and lacked direct communication with the hall above, which was reached by a timber forestair. The arched doorway, secured by a portcullis and draw-bar, gives access to a screens passage at the lower end of an open-roofed hall. Additional living-space of a more private nature is more limited than at Morton, being confined to a single room in an adjacent angle-tower, but there is direct sanitary provision for the hall. The kitchen may have been housed in a timber outbuilding abutting one of the main end-walls.

There is also an interesting series of hall-houses in the west highlands and islands, the earliest of these probably being Skipness, in Kintyre, erected by a member of the MacSween family in about the second quarter of the thirteenth century. Other powerful local families, such as the MacGilchrists, the MacNaughtans and the MacDonalds, soon followed suit and by the end of the century the hall-house had become one of the most popular types of castle in this region. Notable examples occur at Fraoch Eilean, on Loch Awe, and at Ardtornish, in Morvern, while the great hall-house of Aros, on the east coast of Mull, with its massive and lofty walls, huge first-floor hall and well-defended bailey, must have been a princely residence indeed, befitting the status of the MacDougall lords who built it.

Tower-Houses

Although it is impossible now to say how many tower-houses were built in Scotland between the fourteenth and the seventeenth centuries, there is little doubt that surviving structures of this class easily outnumber the combined total of all other types of Scottish castle. The tower-house, of course, is one of the simplest and most basic kinds of fortified residence, and as such was to be found at one time or another in almost every country in western Europe, but in none, with the exception of Ireland, was its popularity so widespread or so long lived as in Scotland.

The popularity of the tower-house in Scotland was due primarily to the fact that, in a society which was economically straitened and politically unstable, it struck just the right balance between the claims of domestic comfort and those of defence. A self-contained residence, it incorporated all the essential ingredients of the normal medieval house in a remarkably compact form and offered a considerable degree of security in return for a fairly modest outlay. Moreover, the plan-form was flexible enough to permit almost endless permutations of scale and detail, allowing both designer and patron to exercise their ingenuity or caprice to the full. Thus, the tower-house was a suitable residence for all ranks of the landowning class, from the King himself who, as late as the 1530s thought fit to erect at the Palace of Holyroodhouse 'ane greit towre to him self to rest into', to the modest Border laird whose tower stood within a farmyard. Furthermore, the architectural and aesthetic qualities of the tower-house admirably expressed the social status of its occupant, the vertical profile and solid stone construction contrasting sharply with the low flimsily-built dwellings of the peasantry. That, once established as the standard type of baron's and gentleman's residence, the tower continued to flourish for so long is best explained by the fact that the economic and social factors that had originally ensured its popularity remained operative, in some parts of the country at least, until well after the Union of the Crowns.

Much the same amount of accommodation was provided in a tower-house as in a hall-house, but it was disposed vertically rather than horizontally, one apartment being placed above another to a height of several storeys; communication between the various rooms was usually obtained by means of a turnpike stair placed in one corner of the building, acting as a vertical corridor. The defensive qualities of the tower were entirely passive, reliance being placed upon the limitation of the ground area to a minimum and upon the construction of thick outer walls, bound together horizontally by one or more barrel-vaults. The entrance itself was often protected by a yett, an outer door comprising a heavy wrought-iron grating of distinctive construction. In the earlier towers only the open parapet, often projected outwards upon stone corbels, allowed the defenders any opportunity for aggressive action, although with the introduction of firearms a variety of gun-loops was frequently provided. Some additional protection was often obtained by the erection of an enclosing courtyard, or barmkin, within which subsidiary buildings and offices were grouped round the tower.

The main stream of development begins with a group of fourteenth- and fifteenth-century towers characterised by their simplicity of plan and massiveness of construction. Most are divided horizontally into two or three principal compartments by barrel-vaults, the uppermost vault supporting a heavy low-pitched roof composed of stone slabs. These structural units are themselves subdivided by partitions and by timber floors, the lowermost compartment invariably being a store-cellar, while

28 Threave Castle,
Kirkcudbrightshire

the one above contains the lord's hall, to which direct external access is usually provided by means of a forestair. Drum Castle admirably illustrates most of these features. The building is of simple rectangular form with slightly rounded corners, and the walls measure up to 12 ft. in thickness. The only original entrance is at first-floor level, giving ready access to the hall and at the same time communicating by means of a mural stair with the basement, whose function as a storage apartment is emphasised by the provision of a well. There is evidence of a small entresol room, perhaps the lord's solar, immediately above the hall, while the upper of the three main barrel-vaulted divisions contains another two floors, one at least of which has extended the full length of the building.

The earliest tower-houses were square or oblong on plan, but it was not long before the advantages of adding one or more wings to the main block came to be appreciated. The resulting variations of plan, and particularly the two main types known as the L-plan and the Z-plan, are sometimes represented primarily as defensive measures, based on the principles that governed the use of flanking towers in the great castles of enclosure. But this is to misunderstand the nature of the balance between defence and amenity in the development of the tower-house for, although the tactical advantages presented by each type of plan were often worked into the general pattern of design, there is little doubt that the main reason for their adoption lay in their contribution to improved standards of domestic comfort and

29 Neidpath Castle, Peeblesshire: plan

efficiency. One of the best examples of the L-plan is Neidpath, erected by one of the Hays of Yester towards the end of the fourteenth century. It has many of the features of the simple oblong towers of the period, but the provision of an additional chamber in the wing at each level makes for a much more flexible plan. Thus, on the first floor the hall occupies the full extent of the main block, having at one end a dais and at the other a screens-passage leading from a kitchen in the adjacent wing. A similar grouping in the basement leaves the whole of the main block free for storage, the wing being occupied by a pit-prison.

The Z-plan, in which two towers were placed at diagonally opposite corners of the main block, went a stage further in solving accommodation problems. This form became especially popular during the later sixteenth century, when the tower-house was entering the final stage of its evolution towards a purely domestic residence. The best known example is Claypotts (1569–88), which incorporates three storerooms and a kitchen on the ground floor, one large apartment in the main block on each of the three upper floors, and no less than eight smaller rooms in the angle-towers.

The L- and Z-forms, although the most frequent were far from being the only variations of plan adopted by designers, and the more exotic deviations

30 Claypotts Castle, Angus

from standard practice include, at one end of the scale, the double-L plan of Borthwick, noblest of all Scottish tower-houses, and at the other the equally unique circular plan of Orchardton, a building of such modest appearance that the lord of Borthwick might well have mistaken it for a dovecot. Nevertheless, the simple oblong tower of primitive aspect never lost its popularity and Coxton (1644), with its stout walls, its ascending sequence of barrel-vaults and its first-floor entrance, looks at first glance like a building of the fifteenth century.

Another way of obtaining more accommodation was to erect additional ranges of buildings inside the barmkin, thus producing a courtyard layout.

31 Borthwick Castle,
Midlothian

This development is well illustrated at Craigmillar, where the original L-plan tower-house of about the late fourteenth century was subsequently enclosed by a strong curtain-wall with corner-towers, buildings being erected round the north, south and west sides of the courtyard thus formed. In the sixteenth century a three-storeyed east range was added, containing kitchens and cellarage on the ground-floor and living-quarters above, while in 1661 the west range was reconstructed to provide a more up-to-date series of principal apartments. At Aldie a similar development can be seen in miniature, buildings of four consecutive periods ranging clockwise round a court only 7ft. square.

No account of the tower-house, however brief, can fail to mention what the late W. D. Simpson termed the 'Indian Summer' of the Scottish Baronial style, the period about the turn of the sixteenth and seventeenth centuries that saw a last vigorous flowering of this essentially vernacular tradition of building. The most notable towers of this era show no novelties of plan, but their elevational treatment is richly varied and their upperworks exhibit an imaginative and profuse display of ornamental detail. Local schools of design can sometimes be distinguished, as for example in Aberdeenshire and in the south-west, where one or two prominent families of master-masons were able to develop recognisable stylistic mannerisms. In the north-east the Bell family of masons was responsible for a small but outstanding group of castles of which the best known are Midmar, Crathes, Fraser and Craigievar. This last, completed by William Forbes in 1626, is perhaps the most remarkable, for no later alterations mar the perfect balance of the elevations or disturb the unity of the original interior decoration. At Craigievar, perhaps more readily than anywhere else in a country whose finest buildings are now often mere empty shells of studiously preserved masonry, it is possible to see a castle as its original occupants saw it and to understand that pride of possession so well expressed by Sir Richard Maitland when he wrote of his own tower of Lethington:

> Thy tour and fortres, lairge and lang,
> Thy neighbours does excell;
> And for thy wallis thick and strang,
> Thou graitly beirs the bell.
> Thy groundis deep, and topis hie,
> Uprising in the air,
> Thy vaultis pleasing are to sie,
> They are so greit and fair.

From Tower-House to Laird's House

During the century and a half following the Reformation the residences of the gentry came to assume a more domestic appearance, but the imprint of the tower-house was slow to disappear. Even in the relatively advanced lowlands the English traveller Thomas Morer, writing in 1689, noted that 'the houses of their quality are high and strong, and appear more like castles

32 Craigievar Castle,
Aberdeenshire

than houses', although he did add that 'now they begin to have better buildings, and to be very modish both in the fabrick and furniture of their dwellings'.

Outwardly, at least, the most noticeable development was a gradual withering away of defensive features. Gun-loops, for instance, tended to be provided more sparingly, and their arrangement frequently suggests that they were designed more for display than for hostile use. Buildings such as Glenbuchat (1590), which incorporates a comprehensive series of enfilading loops, had few successors, the protection of the entrance-doorway by one or two flanking loops, as at Pitreavie, evidently being considered an adequate measure of defence. Killochan (1586), too, has a bare minimum of gun-loops, but in addition there is a corbelled machicolation overlooking the entrance, while at Old Leckie double machicolation, yett and gun-loop guard the entrance, while all other parts are left unprotected. Indeed, it was invariably at the entrance that defensive precautions persisted longest, and the wrought-iron yett remained a standard fitting until about the time of the Civil War, despite periodic attempts at official discouragement such as the Privy Council's decree of 1606 entitled, somewhat optimistically, 'Irone Yettis in the bordouris ordanit to be removit and turnit in plew Irnis'.

No less significant were the developments that were taking place at the wall-head. The earlier towers had open parapet-walks, which were often corbelled out from the wall below and equipped with angle-turrets. The main roof usually rose within the parapet-walk, its heavy covering of stone slabs being partially protected by the battlements. In the post-Reformation tower-house, however, there was an increasing tendency for the open parapet to disappear and for the roof, now invariably a construction of slate and timber, to extend in an unbroken sweep from apex to wall-head, as at Killochan, where there is an enclosed parapet on one side. Angle-turrets, too, were going out of fashion. The primitive open rounds of the early towers had been succeeded by the picturesque conical-roofed 'studies' of the Scottish Baronial style, but even before the end of the sixteenth century some buildings were being constructed with plain gabled roofs. Torwoodhead (1566) provides an early instance of this form, while at Craigston (1604–7) the angle turrets have shrunk to mere corbel-courses and the battlements are represented by an ornamental balcony and mock crenellation. This reluctance to abandon the postures of defence was probably due more to social than to architectural factors, for the castle had always been recognised as a symbol of rank. The point was well made to Lord Lothian by Sir Robert Kerr in 1636, when he wrote to him about proposed improvements at Ancrum House: 'By any meanes do not take away the battlement, as some gave me counsale to do ... for that is the grace of the house, and makes it looke lyk a castle'.

The concern for appearance was reflected in the increased attention given to display and embellishment. The quasi-classical decoration of the dormer-window pediments at Castle Menzies, the Elizabethan pierced

33 Torwood Castle,
Stirlingshire

work at Hill House and the elaborate Anglo-Flemish ornament of Winton
House are all inspired by a common motive. Boldly carved armorial panels
and commemorative inscriptions, too, became an extremely popular means
of adornment at this period. At Castle Menzies the initials and coat of arms
of the laird and his wife appear over the entrance, while further initials and a
pious text are carved on a dormer. Similar examples can be quoted from
every part of the country from Muness (1598), in Shetland, whose builder
was evidently a man of some poetic sensibility:

> List ze to knaw yis bulding quha began
> Laurence the Bruce he was that worthy man
> Quha ernestly his airis and ofspring prayis
> To help and not to hurt this vark aluayis

to Killochan, Ayreshire, whose laird favoured a more matter-of-fact
approach: 'This work was begyn 1 of Marche 1586 be Ihone Cathcart of
Carltovn and Helene Wallace his spous'. The taste for embellishment went
well beyond a concern for the external appearance of a building, however,
for a general increase in the size of window openings and the more frequent

use of glass opened up new opportunities in the field of interior decoration (p. 69).

Important as changes of attitude towards defence and display may have been, the most significant developments in the transition from tower-house to laird's house where those relating to plan-form. The tower-house is, by definition, a structure occupying a very limited surface-area in relation to its height, that is to say it is a tall narrow building in which rooms are placed one above the other. There was, therefore, a limit to the amount of dwelling-space that could be provided and, although problems brought about by steadily rising standards of accommodation had to some extent been met by the introduction of the L- and Z-plans, by the later sixteenth century a point had been reached beyond which further expansion could take place only by means of a fundamental change of plan-form.

The simplest method of obtaining more space was to increase the length of the building, an arrangement well illustrated by the castles of Melgund and Carnasserie. Melgund comprises a four-storeyed L-plan tower-house

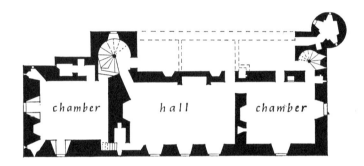

34 Melgund Castle, Angus: plan

with a contemporary two-storeyed wing containing kitchen and storerooms on the ground-floor and a spacious hall and withdrawing-room above. The arrangement at Carnasserie is similar, but at Torwoodhead (1566) there is no distinguishable tower-house, the main block being planned as a single architectural unit.

The same tendency towards horizontal expansion can be observed in later tower-houses of Z-plan. At Glenbuchat the main block, while still containing a single apartment at principal-floor level, is noticeably long in proportion to its breadth, while at Castle Menzies (1577) and Earlshall a further extension of the main block permits two principal apartments to be placed *en suite*, and at Elcho additional towers are introduced to provide more private rooms and better circulation. As greater importance came to be attached to symmetry, however, the Z-plan tended to give way to the half-H plan, in which both wings or angle-towers projected from the same side of the main block rather than from opposite sides.

Craigston furnishes a uniquely compact example of such an arrangement, the two wings being so close together that the space between them can be spanned at eaves-level by an arched balcony. More typical, however, are

Pitreavie and Castle Stewart; in the former the outer walls of the wings are direct extensions of the gable-walls of the main block, while in the latter the wings are set further apart in the manner of angle-towers. Moreover, in each case the symmetry of plan is plainly reflected in the elevations – an indication that master-masons were now beginning to grasp some of the basic principles of Renaissance design. Baberton, erected for his own use by Sir James Murray (p. 73) in 1622–3, follows the same form as Pitreavie and in both buildings extruded circular stair-towers rise within the inner re-entrant angles of main block and wing.

Later in the seventeenth century this type of plan was given more formal expression, as at Culter, near Aberdeen, and Gallery, where the wings begin to assume the character of classical pavilions, such as Sir William Bruce had already introduced in a number of larger houses. Gallery, completed for Sir John Falconer of Balmakellie in 1680 to the design of the Edinburgh master-mason Thomas Wilkie, is a tall building of double-room width with a

35 Gallery House, Angus

central staircase, its name possibly being derived from the handsome long gallery that occupies the first floor of the main block. Occasionally a full H-plan was adopted, as at Bannockburn, a symmetrically planned four-storeyed building in which twin staircases serve a series of well-appointed public and private rooms. The external detail is rather old fashioned, but the elaborate plasterwork of the interiors was probably completed by the English plasterers who had been brought north to work at Holyroodhouse (p. 77).

Conservatism of plan-form was even more marked in the case of the L-plan, whose chief advantages had been exploited as early as the fourteenth century, but which remained in common use until the time of the Union. Among laird's houses that still retain one or two defensive features Castle of Park (1590) shows the L-plan in its simplest form, all the principal apartments being contained within the main block, and the wing being no more than a stair-tower. At Gilbertfield, however, erected some 20 years later, the wing extends beyond the stair and houses additional rooms at each level.

An economical method of increasing the amount of accommodation was to extrude the staircase, the most convenient position for it to occupy being the re-entrant angle formed between main block and wing, where it could provide direct access to rooms in both portions of the building. The staircase could be formed in a number of different ways. During the second half of the sixteenth century it was not uncommon for the lower part of the stair to be enclosed within the wing and for the upper portion alone to be extruded by means of corbelling. This device is seen in its most rudimentary form at Castle of Park itself, while at Braikie (1581) and Killochan the process is carried a stage further. At Braikie a broad turnpike-stair rises within the wing to the first floor, while the remaining levels are reached by means of a much narrower stair corbelled out in the re-entrant angle; the arrangements at Killochan are similar but the lower part of the stair is of the scale-and-platt variety.

One of the most interesting stuctures of this class, and one of the last laird's houses to incorporate specifically defensive features, is Leslie Castle. At first glance the building might be taken for a late-sixteenth-century tower-house, complete with vaulted basement, angle-turrets and a generous

36 Leslie Castle, Aberdeenshire: plan

array of gun-ports. Yet the egg-and-dart ornament of the corbel-courses, the plain gable-copings and the tall diagonally-mounted chimneys clearly point to a later period and there is no reason to doubt the evidence of an inscription which records that the building was founded in 1661. The extruded stair-tower, which rises to the full height of the building, contains a scale-and-platt stair with a hollow newel serving as a heating-duct. With the erection of this businesslike little castle in a remote corner of Aberdeenshire the history of the fortified house in Scotland comes to an end for, as Lord Strathmore wrote of his own stonghold of Castle Lyon (now Castle Huntly) a few years later, 'such houses truly are worn quyt out of fahione, as feuds are, which is a great happiness'.

The typical L-plan laird's house of the mid and late seventeenth century is a plain three- or four-storeyed building having an extruded stair-tower, which contains the main entrance. The tower is commonly of octagonal or circular form, but may also be square, while the stair itself is usually of turnpike construction. Two of the most substantial houses of this class are Hill House, Dunfermline (1623) and Innes (1640–53), where the stair-towers rises to a height of five storeys. The house was designed by the well-known Edinburgh master-mason, William Ayton, one of whose assistants no doubt carved the very modish ornamental detail – an illustration of the way in which the distinctive architectural fashions that had been developed in the great houses of the Lothians might be carried into the provinces.

Another popular layout was the T-plan, a form that was arrived at by throwing out a staircase-wing midway along one side of an elongated tower-house. Crosbie Castle affords a good illustration of this class of building. It rises to a height of three storeys and an attic and the main block is long enough to contain two or more rooms at each level. The central position of the stair makes for exceptionally good circulation, convenient access being provided to rooms at both ends of the house. As in certain L-plan buildings the upper portion of the wing was often given over to living accommodation and the stair itself corbelled out in a re-entrant angle, an arrangement which can be seen at Tullibole (1608) and Old Leckie. One of the most attractive of the smaller houses of this class is Williamstoun, while few can show as well-preserved an internal layout as Pilmuir (1624), where the upper floors contain a fine series of living-rooms, many of which retain their original pine panelling and modelled plasterwork.

One noticeable feature in the later evolution of the tower-house is the increasing extent to which the external elevations came to be regarded as coherent units of design. At first, as at Castle Menzies, this might mean little more than making a half-hearted attempt to introduce some measure of regularity into the disposition of doorway and window openings, but at Newark both front and rear elevations are markedly symmetrical, and the same is true at Duntarvie, where also the entrance is more or less centrally placed. Sometimes the horizontal string-course was employed to unite the various planes of an elevation, as at Innes, where moulded string-courses

37 Innes House,
Morayshire

return round the principal frontage at each storey, binding main block, wing and stair-tower together and at the same time countering the strong vertical thrust of the building.

Most of the earlier tower-houses had been bound together at two or more levels by massive barrel-vaults, a device which made for great structural stability and at the same time afforded some protection against fire. As the defensive role of the tower receded, however, walls were reduced in thickness and vaults used more sparingly, the lowermost storey alone being barrel-vaulted. In post-Reformation times even this precaution was occasionally dispensed with, as at Leckie, where the ground-floor is partly joisted and partly vaulted, while many seventeenth-century laird's houses such as Tullibole and Innes were wholly unvaulted. Whether vaulted or not, however, the ground-floor was invariably used for storage and service purposes, the principal living-rooms being placed at first- and second-floor levels and, so far as larger houses are concerned, this arrangement persisted until the general introduction of the sunk basement in Georgian times.

Courtyard Castles and Palaces
Although most later medieval Scottish castles were tower-houses, a few of the greatest landowners continued to build substantial castles of enclosure whose general form was directly derived from their thirteenth- and fourteenth-century predecessors. By this time, however, the specifically military functions of the castle were beginning to decline throughout Western Europe and these courtyard castles of the later Middle Ages, like their counterparts in other countries, exhibit no new principles of fortification, emphasis being increasingly laid upon the provision of higher standards of domestic accommodation.

Thus at Doune, although careful planning and the immense solidity of the fabric combine to make the castle a most formidable stronghold, the

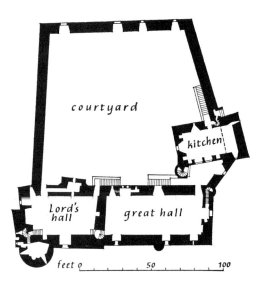

38 Doune Castle, Perthshire: plan

feet 0   50   100

design lacks aggression. Erected as a principal residence of Murdoch, Duke of Albany, Regent of Scotland from 1419 to 1424, the castle was intended to be a structure of unusual size and splendour, comprising four ranges of buildings grouped round a courtyard, but only the north range and part of the west range were completed. The former incorporates two distinct parts, one comprising the gateway with the private rooms of the lord above and the other the great hall with its associated kitchen and service rooms. Apart from arrangements made for safeguarding the entrance the castle relies for its defence chiefly upon its high curtain-wall, which is provided with a continuous parapet-walk and with corbelled rounds at the angles. The design may therefore be regarded as a transitional one, the keep-gatehouse looking back to the thirteenth-century donjon, and the integration of the defensive and domestic arrangements into a regular courtyard-plan anticipating the development of later courtyard-houses and palaces.

The next stage in this development, namely the virtual exclusion of defensive features in return for a more spacious and convenient layout of the residential accommodation, is most clearly seen in the royal palaces of the fifteenth and sixteenth centuries. At Linlithgow a start was made in the 1420s to rebuild an earlier royal castle and by the reign of James V (1513–42) the structure had assumed the quadrangular form that it preserves today. Despite its sprinkling of gun-ports and corbelled parapets Linlithgow is an almost exclusively domestic building. Externally its true character is made clear by the large regularly placed windows, while within there is a well-organised system of communication by means of stairs, corridors and lobbies. The finest of the state apartments is the 'Lion Chalmer' or great hall which, with its adjacent service-rooms and underlying kitchens, occupies the greater part of the east quarter of the palace. A similar pattern can be traced at Edinburgh Castle, where a great hall was erected along one side of Crown Square in about 1500.

Not all late medieval great halls were so readily accommodated, however, and two of the most important examples, situated within the royal castles of Stirling and Falkland respectively, were originally freestanding buildings, although both were subsequently absorbed into rather loose courtyard-plans. The great hall of Stirling, built about the same time as that at Edinburgh, is the finest achievement of late Gothic domestic architecture in Scotland and Defoe went so far as to describe it as 'the noblest I ever saw in Europe'. The plan was fairly orthodox, the hall itself being set over a vaulted basement and having at one end a dais and at the other an entrance-doorway and screens; less usual features included an open gallery running along the principal façade and a private balcony overlooking the body of the hall. The dais was lit by bay-windows ceiled with rib-vaults, the details of the bay designs, like the roof-corbels of the Edinburgh hall, beginning to reflect the influence of the Renaissance. At Falkland the great hall stood on the north side of the palace, but only the foundations remain to show its general resemblance to the Stirling hall.

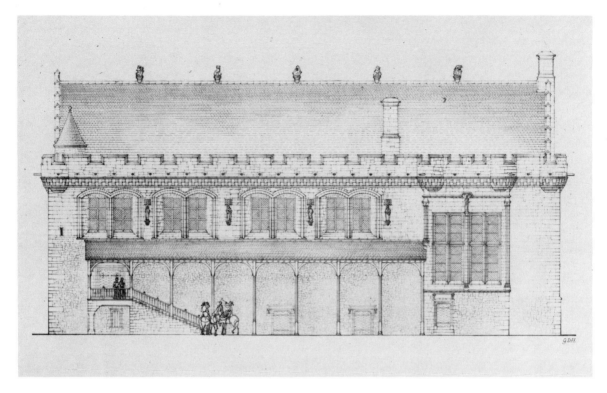

39 Great Hall, Stirling
Castle

The activities of the designers of the Royal Works were intensified during
the later reign of James V, a period which saw a sustained programme of
royal building on a scale unparalleled in Scottish architectural history. The
early stages of this programme, involving the building of the Great Tower
and principal quadrangle of the palace of Holyroodhouse (p. 48), were
carried out by local master-masons working in the vernacular idiom. With
the renewal of the Franco-Scottish alliance in 1537 through the king's
marriage policies, however, steps were at once taken to secure the
appointment of selected French master-craftsmen to high office in the Royal
Works and the new arrivals were not slow in making their presence felt.
Extensive building operations were undertaken in 1537–41 at Falkland,
where the courtyard façades of the palace, in which the bays are defined by
buttresses modelled as classical columns and incorporate medallion busts,
are clearly of French derivation and can probably be attributed to the two
French master-masons whose names appear in the building accounts. In
contrast to the arrangements at Falkland, where most of the emphasis is
placed upon the courtyard façades, the palace of Stirling (1540–2) is a
completely outward-looking building, the inner elevations being treated
very simply but the external ones with great elaboration. Yet the
symmetrical division of the external elevations into recessed bays, each
containing a sculptured figure set upon a baluster-shaft, is no less French in
inspiration even although the sculptures themselves are derived from
German engravings. Within there is a fine suite of state rooms on the first

floor, although little now remains of their fittings apart from some handsome chimney-pieces and a number of ceiling medallions (the 'Stirling Heads') which are probably the finest examples of Scottish Renaissance wood-carving now extant.

The façades of the royal palaces of Falkland and Stirling were among the earliest attempts at coherent Renaissance design in Britain, yet they had few successors and exerted no general influence. For the rest of the sixteenth century Scottish architecture remained obstinately Scottish, classical motifs penetrating only as decorative ingredients in an essentially vernacular style of building, while the few buildings whose designs reflect foreign influences, such as Drochil (c. 1578) and Crichton (p. 69), are of interest chiefly as curiosities.

Artillery Fortifications

Cannon were probably employed against the Scots as early as Edward II's invasion of 1327, but it was not until about the middle of the following century that the Scottish royal army itself seems to have been equipped with effective ordnance, most of the pieces, like the celebrated Mons Meg, no

40 Falkland Palace, Fife

doubt being of foreign manufacture. Defence against such weapons was at first very much a matter of improvisation. Because artillery had a lower trajectory and greater penetrating power than the traditional siege-engine, walls came to be reduced in height and thickened. After the siege of Tantallon in 1528, for example, instructions were given to block up all apertures in the curtain-wall, while during the construction of the Half Moon Battery at Edinburgh Castle in 1574 the fourteenth-century David's Tower was lowered in height, packed with rubble and encased in the new work. Provision for the defensive use of firearms, too, was initially obtained by the adaptation of existing methods of fortification. Thus, the customary archers' firing slits in walls and towers began to be replaced by openings designed to house small cannon or hand-guns, the earliest examples usually being of 'inverted key-hole' shape. During the sixteenth century horizontal wide-mouthed gun-ports came into fashion, to be joined as the century progressed by numerous other varieties, some evidently designed to accommodate hack-buts and pistols.

Many castles of the period incorporate such gun-loops, but few have any comprehensively designed scheme of defence. A particularly notable exhibition of strength occurs at Noltland, where the many tiers of horizontal gun-ports give the structure something of the appearance of a naval man-of-war. One of the first Scottish buildings to be designed specifically with the new arm in mind was the royal castle of Ravenscraig, Fife (begun 1460), where a promontory site is straddled by a curtain-wall and terminal D-shaped towers, all of unusually massive construction. The towers and the lower parts of the curtain are equipped with inverted key-hole gun-ports, while the upper portion of the curtain carries a later artillery-platform with wide-mouthed ports. James IV's Forework at Stirling Castle shows little novelty, but Craignethan, reconstructed by Sir James Hamilton of Finnart in 1532–40, had a curtain no less than 16ft. in thickness and beyond it a broad flat-bottomed ditch containing a loopholed traverse and a caponier which must have been one of the first of its kind in Britain.

These early artillery works, like their counterparts in other countries, involved no radical departure from medieval methods of fortification, but the invention of a new type of angular bastion in Italy early in the sixteenth century soon led to revolutionary developments. Such bastions, specifically designed to mount artillery, usually took the form of solid straight-sided earthen platforms having external revetments of timber or masonry. At Dunbar Castle the Regent Albany employed a foreign designer to erect a massive casemated block-house of angular plan in about 1520, while 30 years later a series of regular earthwork forts were built in south-east Scotland by English and Italian engineers in an attempt to consolidate the gains made by Somerset's armies.

Little now remains of these, or of the much larger bastioned citadels that subsequently marked the Cromwellian occupation, while the little fort at

Lerwick, erected under the direction of John Mylne to protect Bressay Sound during the Dutch War of 1665–7, was largely reconstructed in the eighteenth century, when it was renamed Fort Charlotte. In the highlands internal dissension for a time presented as great a threat as foreign invasion. Already at the end of Charles II's reign there had been a project for strengthening the defences of Stirling by the erection of a powerful artillery-fort at the north end of Stirling Bridge. Although this came to nothing a new fort, named Fort William, was constructed at Inverlochy in 1692, while in the period between the two Jacobite rebellions a comprehensive programme for the pacification of the highlands was carried out using the same methods that had enabled the Roman armies to subjugate lowland Scotland 1500 years previously. Roads and bridges were built where they had never been built before, garrison posts were established at strategic

41 Fort George, Inverness-shire

points, the defences of existing castles were improved, and two new major forts, Fort Augustus and Fort George, were erected on the line of the Great Glen.

Fort George, at Ardersier Point, was begun soon after the Forty-five and completed in about 1769 under the direction of Colonel William Skinner. The plan is adapted to the converging promontory-site, the main weight of the defence being concentrated upon the landward side, where the principal curtain-wall and angle-bastions are strengthened by a broad ditch and ravelin; the works occupy an area of some 16 acres and the plain well-proportioned barrack-blocks contain accommodation for about 2000 men. The fort has recently been skilfully restored and its excellent state of preservation and well-documented record of construction combine to make it one of the most interesting examples of Hanoverian artillery fortification in the British Isles.

3
Early Classicism

The Great Courtyard Houses of the Nobility

By the time that James VI ascended the English throne in 1603 the architectural initiative had already passed from the Crown to the nobility and the departure of the Court to Whitehall set the seal on this development. There was now less need for the King's Masters of Works to undertake expensive new building-projects at the royal castles and palaces, for James made only a single brief visit to Scotland after the Union while his son came only to be crowned. The nobles, however, still for the most part secure upon their estates and at last beginning to enjoy the benefits of stable government, had both the incentive and the means to build.

Many great landholders, of course, such as the Hamiltons and the Douglas Earls of Morton, were content to go on living in the tower-houses and castles of their forebears, perhaps adding a new wing or refurbishing a suite of rooms as a concession to changing fashions. Some of these projects, although small in scale, were varied and novel. At Crichton the Earl of Bothwell rebuilt the north range of the castle in the late 1580s, introducing a handsome scale-and-platt staircase (one of the first in Scotland) and a remarkable courtyard façade, both in the Italian manner. At Huntly, Aberdeenshire, in contrast, Elizabethan and French late-Gothic elements predominate in the richly decorated show-front contrived for the 1st Marquess of Huntly in 1602.

Of those who built sizeable new houses the majority favoured the well-tried courtyard layout, increasing importance now being attached, however, to the achievement of symmetry both in plan and elevation. Considerations of security could by this time usually be disregarded, but certain defensive features, such as gun-ports, draw-bars and vaulted undercrofts, persisted for a remarkably long time.

Fashions in decoration also changed at this period, the Scottish Baronial manner gradually being superseded by a new and equally distinctive style, ultimately derived from books and engravings published in the Low Countries, but reaching Scotland in a digested form evolved in Elizabethan England. This Anglo-Netherlandish ornament, with its elaborate cartouches and grotesques, and intricately-patterned strapwork, was employed both for external and for internal decoration, one of the earliest known examples of its use being in a painted ceiling of 1581 formerly at

Prestongrange. It was not until the first two decades of the seventeenth century that the new style became fashionable, however, its rapid dissemination being promoted both by the introduction of English craftsmen and by the direct importation of English workshop-products.

As part of the preparations made for James VI's visit of 1617, for example, the Privy Council commissioned two leading London craftsmen, Nicholas Stone and Matthew Goodrich, to supply a screen, stalls and other furnishings for the Chapel Royal at Holyroodhouse, since 'this work could not be gottin so perfytlie and well done within this cuntrey as is requisite'. These have long since disappeared, but another major work almost certainly of London manufacture, the elaborate marble monument (c. 1611) to the Earl of Dunbar in Dunbar Parish Church, survives to illustrate the kind of model that now became available to Scottish masons and carvers.

Perhaps the most noticeable development in the sphere of interior decoration that took place during the years following the Union of the Crowns was the introduction of modelled plasterwork of Elizabethan type. Compartmented ceilings of geometric pattern with moulded cornices and enriched friezes, and massive overmantels often incorporating coats of arms and life-size figures, now began to appear in Scotland. Among the earlier examples mention should be made of a remarkable group of ceilings in the Edinburgh area, including those at Pinkie, Winton and the Binns, and of a second series in the north east, likewise the products of a single team of craftsmen, of which the most outstanding are at the castles of Muchalls and Craigievar. Most of the plasterers were probably English and there is evidence to suggest that some at least of them came from London and others from York. Despite the popularity of ornamental plasterwork, painted decoration remained fashionable, being used both in conjunction with other materials, for example to heighten the effect of carved woodwork, and as a sole medium, as in the ceiling of the long gallery at Pinkie. Most painted decoration was executed by native craftsmen, but one or two English painters are also known to have been employed.

One of the finest courtyard buildings of this period is the Earl's Palace, Kirkwall, erected soon after 1600 by Patrick Stewart, Earl of Orkney, a notorious local despot. The accommodation, which is exceptionally well planned, includes a suite of three principal apartments on the first floor, approached by a spacious scale-and-platt staircase. Much use is made of oriel- and bay-windows, the whole being lavishly ornamented in a style akin to that seen at Huntly. More interesting, perhaps, as a forerunner of a type of building that was later to become fashionable, was the nearby palace at Birsay. This 'sumptuous and stately dwelling' was commenced by Earl Patrick's no less tyrannical father, Robert, Earl of Orkney, a natural son of James V, as early as 1574, the original building apparently forming three sides of a large oblong courtyard having square angle-pavilions and an axially-placed entrance. The structure is now a mere shell, but early drawings show that the symmetry of the plan was reflected in the elevations,

42 Painted Ceiling,
Delgatie Castle,
Aberdeenshire

which incorporated a generous array of windows and prominently-ranged chimney-stacks.

A somewhat similar design of even more ambitious conception was adopted by Sir John Seton of Barnes, one of James VI's courtiers, in the early 1590s. Here the pavilioned forecourt fronts a symmetrically-planned house of pure Elizabethan type, complete with flanking wings, extruded staircase-towers and a central entrance giving on to a scale-and-platt stair. It seems almost certain that Sir John obtained his plan from an English architect, and influences from the same quarter are clearly discernible at another Seton house in the Lothians, Pinkie, which was enlarged and remodelled for the Earl of Dunfermline during the second decade of the

43 Earl's Palace, Kirkwall, Orkney

seventeenth century. Lord Hay, too, for a time contemplated re-building his neighbouring seat of Yester along Elizabethan lines, while Viscount Stormont's palace of Scone, evidently one of the most magnificent houses of its day, appears to have incorporated a number of English features.

One characteristic feature of great houses such as these, however, namely the long gallery, cannot claim the English parentage that is often foisted upon it. Galleries are known to have existed in Scotland as early as the fifteenth century, and the royal palaces of Holyrood and Falkland both possessed sizeable long galleries by the reign of James V. During the last quarter of the sixteenth century they began to appear in private houses, and notable examples of this period may be seen at Tolquhon and Dunottar. Galleries also remained fashionable much longer in Scotland than they did in England, those at Hamilton (p. 85) and Mountstuart (p. 88) being among the last to be erected.

In those cases where substantial portions of an older fabric were retained, as at Rowallan Castle, the layout of the courtyard inevitably tended to be irregular, while at Caerlaverock Castle (p. 45) and at Seton House (now destroyed) the disposition of earlier buildings imposed a triangular plan. For new houses, however, a layout based upon a hollow square with corner pavilions was more often adopted, some of the largest mansions of the seventeenth century being erected on this plan.

The earliest of these appears to have been Abbey House, Culross, built in 1608 for Edward Bruce, Lord Kinloss, a prominent figure at the Jacobean court. The building was never completed and only a fragment remains today, but this is sufficient to show that the principal front, originally some 200 feet in length, was divided longitudinally by a spine-wall to house two sets of rooms within its width, a refinement of planning hitherto rare in Scotland. Unlike Birsay and Barnes the building appears to have been unvaulted and without defensive provisions such as gun-loops. The elevations, whose appearance is preserved in early views, incorporated two rows of symmetrically-disposed windows, those on the first floor having pilastered jambs and triangular pediments with thistle finials. The horizontal character of the elevations was further emphasised by prominent string-courses at first-floor and eaves levels.

Many of the features found in Lord Kinloss's house soon re-appeared elsewhere. Thus, the elevations, and perhaps also the plan, of the great mansion built by Lord Dunbar within the walls of Berwick Castle shortly before his death in 1611 had elements that strongly recall Abbey House. The architect was James Murray, a master-wright who had recently been appointed Master of the King's Works, and who seems to have been a figure of some importance in Scottish architecture during the years following the Union of the Crowns. Indeed, it is not unlikely that Murray himself had furnished the designs for Lord Kinloss's house, while he must certainly have been largely responsible for two buildings of similar style erected a few years later by the Royal Works in connection with James VI's visit of 1617. Here, in the King's Lodgings at Edinburgh Castle and in the north quarter of Linlithgow Palace the double-pile plan and proto-classical elevations of Abbey House re-appear, the ornamental detail now being thoroughly Anglo-Flemish in character.

Some credit for the design of the new lodgings at Edinburgh and Linlithgow should probably also be given to the King's Master-Mason,

William Wallace, whose evident skill as a carver may well have been matched by his proficiency as a devisor of buildings. The best-known work with which Wallace's name can be associated, however, and one that well illustrates the mixed ancestry of the Scottish Renaissance style, is Heriot's Hospital, Edinburgh, begun in 1628 but not completed until the end of the century. In this case the main features of the symmetrical courtyard plan probably derive from an Italian pattern-book, but their translation into three-dimensional form was undertaken by a succession of native master-masons, of whom Wallace was the first. In general the elevations follow the lines laid down at Abbey House, Culross, but the mock-castellated superstructure of the corner pavilions looks back to the Baronial style, while the Gothic windows of the chapel reflect the even more conservative outlook of Scottish post-Reformation church architecture. The boldly-carved ornamental detail is Netherlandish.

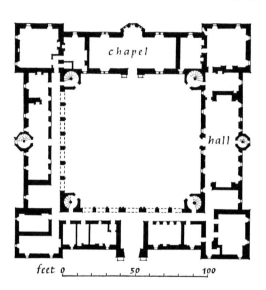

44 Heriot's Hospital, Edinburgh: plan

Curiously enough the same plan had been utilised ten years previously by the designer, perhaps Wallace himself, who prepared a scheme for remodelling Drumlanrig Castle for Sir William Douglas, later 1st Earl of Queensberry. The project seems to have got no further at this stage, but in 1679 it was revived by the 1st Duke who proceeded not only to make use of his grandfather's plans but to execute them in what must for the most part have been a consciously archaic manner. The result is a building almost identical to Heriot's Hospital in plan and massing, but embodying an exuberant classical show-front, complete with double circular staircase, giant Corinthian order and a central entrance-porch supporting a clock-tower capped by a huge ducal coronet. The design evidently derives from Sir William Bruce's west front at Holyroodhouse (p. 77), and indirectly from France, while the lavish ornamental detail, some of it the work of two Dutch carvers brought up from London by the Duke, contains both Caroline and

Gothic elements. The architect appears to have been the young James
Smith, then on the threshold of his career, and although his design displays
considerable uncertainty in the employment of the classical vocabulary the
overall effect is one of immense dignity and splendour, a unique alliance of
the castellated and Renaissance styles in which Scottish Baronial is
unexpectedly translated into baroque.

45 Drumlanrig Castle,
Dumfriesshire

Sir William Bruce and his Circle

When building activity was resumed in Scotland after the Civil War it was
again the nobility who took the lead, particularly those whose prominence
in public affairs brought them into close contact with the English court.
Noblemen of Charles II's day were better educated than their parents and
grandparents, however, and took a more informed interest in architecture
and the allied arts. Many had travelled abroad, the older ones perhaps as
soldiers or political exiles, the younger generation more probably as

students, sent by their parents to spend two or three years in the fashionable academies of Holland or France. Some of the more enlightened members of the aristocracy such as the 1st Marquess of Tweeddale, who was described by Evelyn as 'a learned and knowing nobleman', even found time to cultivate academic and scientific pursuits, while books on architecture and planting began to appear in country-house libraries in increasing numbers. It is not surprising to find, therefore, that designers now emerged from within the ranks of the landed classes to challenge the pre-eminence formerly enjoyed in this sphere by master-craftsmen.

Of these 'gentlemen architects' the foremost was unquestionably Sir William Bruce, who must be accounted the founder of the classical school in Scotland, as well as a pioneer in planting and garden design. The younger son of a small Fife laird, Bruce was born in or about 1630. Almost nothing is known of his early life, although it is possible that he attended St Andrews University for a short time in early youth. His family were strong royalists, and by taking an active part in the negotiations that immediately preceded the Restoration Bruce appears to have come to the personal notice of Charles II and his principal Scottish lieutenant, the (future) Duke of Lauderdale, thus setting his feet firmly on the ladder of political promotion.

A knighthood and baronetcy quickly followed, together with a succession of minor but lucrative official appointments, and Bruce was soon able to establish himself as a landed proprietor in Fife and Kinross-shire. In 1671 Lauderdale also obtained for him the Surveyorship of the King's Works in Scotland, although this office was abruptly terminated in 1678 following the withdrawal of the Duke's friendship. Bruce succeeded in maintaining his position up to the end of Charles II's reign, however, by which time he was a member of the Scottish Privy Council, and if contemporary rumour is to be believed, within sight of a much-coveted viscountcy. His public career came to an end shortly afterwards, however, when he failed to survive the political manoeuvrings that followed the accession of James II, while after the Revolution Settlement of 1689 Bruce's Jacobite and Episcopalian sympathies increasingly set him at odds with the government, leading to his enforced confinement on more than one occasion. He suffered other disappointments, too, during the last years of his life, including bereavement and family estrangement, while a mounting burden of debt made it impossible for him to complete the great mansion at Kinross which he had begun in more prosperous days. Bruce died at a very advanced age on New Year's Day 1710 and was buried in the family vault at Kinross.

There is little direct evidence to show how Bruce acquired his knowledge of architecture, but it seems likely that an inherent interest in the subject was developed both by theoretical studies and by travel. As well as visiting the Low Countries shortly before the Restoration he is known to have made a 'foreign journey' on Lauderdale's behalf in 1663. Bruce also travelled a good deal in England and knew London well, and these journeys would have enabled him to acquire that close acquaintance with the works of

Hugh May and Roger Pratt that is so closely reflected in his own buildings. With a third leading architect of the English Caroline school, William Samwell, he had more direct contacts, and Bruce's association with Samwell in the remodelling of Ham House for the Lauderdales in 1671–5 may well have been a major factor in the development of his later career. It is also clear that Bruce made good use of such architectural treatises as were available, and his booksellers' accounts include the works of Palladio, Vignola and Fréart, as well as others dealing with fortification, engraving and land-surveying.

Most of Bruce's designs were for the country houses of relatives or friends, the only major project that he undertook in his capacity as Surveyor being the reconstruction of the palace of Holyroodhouse in 1671–9, a scheme which appears to have owed more to Lauderdale's initiative than to the enthusiasm of Charles II himself, who never returned to Scotland after the Restoration. A complete rebuilding operation was ruled out by shortage of funds, so Bruce accepted the stylistic anomalies of the old palace and contrived a new façade by erecting a replica of James V's tower-house to counter-balance the original, and linked them together by means of a low balustraded screen and portico, all very much in the French manner. At the same time the principal quadrangle was remodelled to house a new series of state apartments, the pure if restrained classicism of the main elevations introducing a completely new idiom into Scottish architecture. The interiors were richly decorated in the latest style by English and Dutch craftsmen, some of whom were being employed concurrently by Lauderdale and Bruce in their own building operations.

In his private works, too, Bruce at first had to be content to remodel existing buildings rather than to design new ones. Indeed, at Leslie House, rebuilt by his old friend and neighbour the Earl of Rothes in 1667–72, Bruce's advice seems to have been sought only with regard to interior decoration and the layout of the gardens, the replanning of the house itself being left to the King's Master-Mason, John Mylne, and his nephew and successor in office, Robert Mylne. At Balcaskie (1668–76), a small estate in the East Neuk of Fife which Bruce had purchased in 1665, there was already an adequate dwelling-house of fairly recent date. Rather than pull this down and start afresh, therefore, he made it the centrepiece of an axially-planned courtyard layout, complete with concave screen-walls, classical service-wings and terminal vistas, a distinctly novel conception in Restoration Scotland, but one to which Bruce was to return more than once in later years. Local craftsmen were employed for the most part, but for the redecoration of the principal apartments George Dunsterfield, an English plasterer, was brought across from Holyroodhouse, to be followed shortly afterwards by the Dutch painter Jacob de Wet.

By this time Bruce was deeply involved in the building operations being carried out by the Duke and Duchess of Lauderdale both at Ham House and at their three Scottish seats. The Duchess, who was a cousin of Bruce's on her mother's side, had consulted him about the design of a gateway at Ham in 1671, shortly before her marriage to Lauderdale brought the property under the Duke's control. Bruce arranged to have the gatepiers quarried and cut by Robert Mylne at Longannet, on the River Forth, whence they were shipped to Richmond. Three similar gateways were supplied four years later, as well as a consignment of 'Scotch marble' chimney-pieces and a number of garden statues, some of which Bruce appears to have obtained from Holland.

Mylne also acted as master-mason at Thirlestane Castle, the Duke's principal Scottish house, where Bruce enlarged and remodelled the late medieval tower-house (1670–6), introducing a symmetrical forecourt layout similar in conception to the one at Balcaskie. The best of the Holyroodhouse plasterers were employed to redecorate the state rooms, while among the joiners and painters were several highly-skilled Dutch craftsmen apparently recruited at Ham House. Further additions were

46 Thirlestane Castle, Berwickshire: Plasterwork

proposed and partially executed at Thirlestane in about 1680, some of them closely reflecting Samwell's work at Ham, but by this time Bruce had fallen from the Duke's favour and the extent of his involvement is uncertain. Simple axial planning was also the keynote of Bruce's schemes for remodelling Brunstane (1672–4) and Lethington (1672–7, now called Lennoxlove), but at neither house was work fully completed.

Bruce's first opportunity to build an entirely new house on a clear site came in 1676, when the 1st Marquess of Atholl asked him to prepare plans for a small country mansion at Dunkeld (pulled down in 1830). The resulting design was clearly based upon the compact 'oblong square' type of plan that had been developed by English architects such as May and Samwell. A hip-roofed block comprising a basement, two principal storeys and an attic, the house was nearly square on plan, being divided on its short axis into three main portions by thick partition-walls containing the chimney-flues. Externally the house was very plain, the most distinctive features being the small widely-spaced windows, the low attic storey and prominent chimney-stacks and cupola, all except this last probably deriving from one of the plates in Rubens' *Palazzi di Genova*.

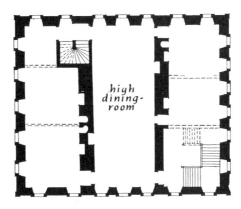

47 Moncreiffe House, Perthshire: plan

Bruce used an almost identical design a year or two later at Moncreiffe (destroyed by fire in 1957), but for his own house at Kinross (1679–93) he employed a 'double-pile' plan such as Pratt had used at Coleshill, that is to say one in which an oblong block of double-room width was bisected on its long axis by a central corridor. The treatment of the elevations follows that of Dunkeld and Moncreiffe, but the attic is still further suppressed, its windows (those in the centre formerly helping to light a 'double-cube' saloon) peeping out between the cornice and the overhanging eaves of the great undormered roof. All the exposed masonry is of warm-coloured sandstone ashlar expertly cut and laid under the direction of the Alloa master-mason Tobias Bachop, and there is also some spirited relief-carving by James Mercer of St Andrews. The interior decoration is in the Anglo-Dutch style that Bruce himself had been instrumental in introducing to Scotland, but money was lacking to finish the upper floors as lavishly as he wished. No expense was spared, however, in creating an appropriate setting for the house, and the well-integrated layout of forecourts, gardens and policies (now partly restored) demonstrates Bruce's mastery of formal planning on the grand scale.

Although none of Bruce's later houses could quite match the serene dignity of Kinross, a number of important works were executed during the last decade or so of his life. At Craigiehall (1698–9) he produced a more sophisticated version of the compact type of house with which he had first experimented in the 1670s, while the subtly-modelled façade of Mertoun (1703–9, formerly known as Harden), like Craigiehall a product of his partnership with Tobias Bachop, reveals his inventive faculties quite undiminished by age. The plan of Mertoun was a reduced version of that of Kinross with a similar arrangement of mezzanine rooms on the principal floor. Hopetoun (1699–1703), the grandest of Bruce's country houses, was a more complex design comprising a centrally-planned main block with angle-pavilions linked by convex screen-walls to terminal office-wings. French influence is apparent in the horizontal rustication of the principal façade (the mason-work again by Bachop) and in the bold semicircular pediment of the garden front, while for the side elevations Bruce went back

48 Kinross House, Kinross-shire

to his Craigiehall design with its distinctive two-window pedimented centrepiece.

49 Kinross House, Kinross-shire: Drawing-room

In the shaping of the gardens and policies of Hopetoun Bruce was assisted by one of his most talented protégés, Alexander Edward, whose career deserves some notice in its own right. Edward was a Scots minister's son from Angus who, after graduating at St Andrews University in 1670, himself entered the church, holding the living of Kemback, Fife, until 'outed' as a non-juror in 1689. As well as sharing his father's historical and scientific tastes Edward developed a keen interest in architecture and planting, his earliest recorded activity in this field being the preparation of drawings of Kinross House and policies for Sir William Bruce in about 1684. No doubt his association with Bruce stood him in good stead after the Revolution Settlement, when he decided to make a career for himself as an architect and garden designer, and he soon acquired a wide clientele among the nobility and gentry, more particularly those of Jacobite persuasion.

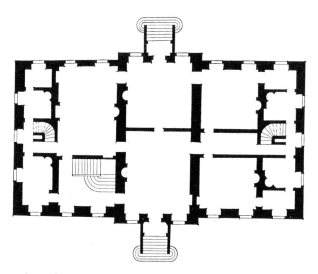

50 Mertoun House,
Berwickshire: plan

Edward was also in close touch with leading Scottish *cognoscenti* such as
Robert Wodrow, James Sutherland (first superintendent of the Edinburgh
Botanic Garden) and Sir Robert Sibbald, who later paid tribute to him as a
'Great Master in Architecture, and contrivance of Avenues, Gardens and
Orchards'.

In 1701 two of his principal patrons, the Earls of Panmure and Mar, with
others of their circle, provided funds for Edward to travel in England,
France and the Low Countries in order to obtain trees and plants for them,
and 'for viewing, observing and taking draughts of the most curious and
remarkable houses, edifices, gardings, orchards, parks, plantations, land
improvements', etc. On his return Edward was to give each of his sponsors
three drawings of their choice and spend three days a year with each of them
in an advisory capacity for up to three years. Only one of his drawings
appears to survive – a plan of Marly now in the Gibbs collection – but his
travel notes and letters reveal an acquisitiveness for botanical specimens,
architectural books and engravings, scientific instruments, and natural
curiosities of all kinds, which cannot have failed to delight his patrons.

Edward's death at a comparatively early age in 1708 evidently cut short a

51 Hopetoun House,
West Lothian

promising career, and his recorded works are few. The most notable project with which his name can be associated was the remodelling of Brechin Castle for the 4th Earl of Panmure, a difficult client who had fallen out with his previous architectural advisor James Bain, the King's Master-Wright, after several years of fruitless building-activity. Edward's local connections probably helped to establish him in the Earl's favour, and from about 1695 onwards he began to prepare schemes for a formal courtyard-layout with twin pavilions and both axial and radial avenues, all very much after the model of Kinross. The castle itself was also replanned along more convenient lines and provided with a symmetrical façade (not completed until 1711), more pedestrian perhaps than Bruce would have contrived, but not without dignity. Edward also produced a most interesting series of garden designs for the neighbouring castle of Kinnaird, belonging to the 4th Earl of Southesk, while at the time of his death he was busy preparing an ambitious scheme for the policies of Hamilton Palace, recently rebuilt to the designs of James Smith.

Apart from Bruce himself Smith was easily the most distinguished figure in Scottish architecture during the period between the Restoration and the

52 Brechin Castle, Angus

death of George II. Born in 1644/5 James Smith was the son of a prominent Forres master-mason of the same name who had married the daughter of a local public notary. Of his education and training little is known beyond the evidence of his own statement, in which he claimed to have had a 'liberal education at schools and colledges at home and abroad and occasion to know the world by travelling abroad', but family tradition held that he had been destined for the church and had subsequently studied architecture in Italy. Smith first comes on record in 1677 as one of the master-masons engaged upon the reconstruction of Holyroodhouse under the direction of Sir William Bruce and Robert Mylne. Thereafter promotion was rapid, for after becoming an Edinburgh burgess two years later by virtue of his marriage to Mylne's eldest daughter he was in 1683 appointed Overseer of the Royal Works in Scotland, the post formerly held by Bruce. Smith appears to have owed this appointment to the recommendation of Lord Queensberry, for whom he was at that time remodelling Drumlanrig. Little need be said here about his career as Surveyor, for there was not much royal building in Scotland at this period, Smith's most important undertaking in this capacity, apart from the refitting of the Chapel Royal, being in connection with the construction and maintenance of the various Highland garrisons and forts in the years after the Union (p. 67).

His official duties being relatively light, Smith was able to build up an extensive private practice as an architect and building contractor and this, together with the success of various business enterprises in which he engaged, soon enabled him to purchase the small estate of Whitehill, near Musselburgh, his establishment as a landed proprietor being marked by a grant of arms and by appointments as a Commissioner of Supply and JP. He also held property in Forres and represented the burgh in parliament in 1685–6, but an attempt to re-enter politics as MP for Edinburgh 30 years later proved unsuccessful. Although dismissed from the Surveyorship in 1719 after 36 years' service Smith kept his architectural and business practices going, in partnership with Alexander McGill until the failure of a colliery enterprise brought financial ruin and forced him to sell Whitehill. He died in 1731 at the age of 86, a reputed Roman Catholic and the father, on his own testimony, of 32 children, one at least of whom was a mason. Smith's principal architectural assistants, apart from McGill, were his two young cousins and former apprentices James and Gilbert Smith, who later became his brothers-in-law through the architect's second marriage to their sister Anne. The younger James Smith (d. 1705) also carried on business on his own account, mainly in Edinburgh, while Gilbert (d. 1726) was appointed King's Master Mason in Scotland in 1715.

Smith, like Bruce, found his greatest opportunities in designing and remodelling country houses, a task to which he brought a sound practical knowledge of the building trade as well as special abilities as a mason and sculptor. Apart from Drumlanrig, where he had to work within the limits of a predetermined scheme, his earliest major undertaking was probably his own house at Whitehill (c. 1690, now known as New Hailes), which was a simplified version of the compact hip-roofed type of house introduced by Bruce at Dunkeld. Similar designs were adopted a few years later by both Bruce (at Hill of Tarvit and Auchindinny) and Smith (at Raith) and proved so successful that they were subsequently reproduced in countless laird's houses of the Georgian period.

By this time the Smiths were also busily engaged upon an important project at Hamilton, where they had taken on the job of converting the old palace into a fashionable mansion of the first rank (demolished c. 1929). James Smith had, in fact, been asked to prepare designs for this as early as 1682, but it was not until ten years later that the Duke and Duchess of Hamilton at last made up their minds to start building, and then only after consulting Sir William Bruce, who was by now recognised as the doyen of Scottish architects. The final scheme, which owed a good deal to the Hamiltons themselves, was a piecemeal one, involving the successive reconstruction of three of the original four courtyard-ranges to form a half-H-plan building incorporating an elaborate porticoed centrepiece. For the courtyard elevations Smith and his cousin of the same name produced a very French-looking but somewhat old-fashioned design with pedimented dormer-windows and ornamental lead flashing on the roof – a favourite device of the Smiths. This seems to have been modified, however, after the elder Smith had been packed off to Hampton Court to consult Wren's surveyor Matthew Banckes, whom the Duke declared to be 'the best at contriving of any in England', and who himself contributed a number of drawings. When the scheme for the portico was under consideration in 1696 advice was again sought from Wren's circle, but Smith claimed full credit for the final design which, although marred by a number of structural peculiarites, effectively signalized the introduction of the full-scale temple front into Scotland. The interiors were handsomely decorated in the English taste, one of their most notable features being a series of carved chimney-pieces and overmantels by William Morgan, who had been brought up from London for the fitting out of the Chapel Royal (p. 93), and who was subsequently associated with many of the Smiths' most important undertakings.

From Hamilton the Smiths moved almost at once to Dalkeith (1701–10) to begin the remodelling and enlargement of the old Douglas Castle for the widowed Duchess of Monmouth and Buccleuch, who had now decided to return to Scotland after long residence in the south. Again a variety of plans were considered, including one for a completely new house, but in the end the Duchess fixed upon a scheme for a half-H-plan building very similar in conception to Hamilton. Smith handled the Dalkeith design with much greater assurance, however, skilfully disguising the irregularities of the old building and grouping the new wings and pavilions so as to achieve a most effective recession from the temple front. The interiors were even more sumptuously decorated than those at Hamilton, with much use of glass and

53 Dalkeith House, Midlothian

marble, inlaid floors and some fine carving by William Morgan and Grinling Gibbons, including a number of items brought up by the Duchess from Moor Park; the total cost exceeded £16000.

When it came to building new houses Smith found little more opportunity for originality than he had in remodelling old ones, a state of affairs which evidently owed more to the conservatism of his clients than to any lack of invention on the architect's part. Thus, at Melville (1697–1701) a markedly Italianate design which he prepared for Lord Melville's consideration was rejected, together with schemes by Sir William Bruce and others, in favour of a taller but more compact version of the type of English country house characterized by Belton. At Yester (1699–1729), where he worked in partnership with McGill, Smith produced a plan not unlike that of Kinross, while the horizontal rustication of the principal elevations strongly recalls Hopetoun and Mertoun. One unusual feature of the interior, however, was that the central hall and saloon rose to a height of two storeys, the hall being galleried, but this arrangement did not survive the subsequent reconstruction of the house by William Adam.

Although Smith's executed works stamp him as a follower of Sir William Bruce, some of his recently-discovered drawings reveal him in another and quite unexpected role as a pioneer of British Palladianism. Whether these remarkable Italianate designs were the product of first-hand knowledge or of theoretical study is not yet clear, and their Palladian theme was exploited not by Smith himself but by his fellow-countryman Colin Campbell, into whose possession the drawings appear to have come about the time that the latter abandoned his career as a Scots lawyer in order to set up as an architectural publicist and designer in London. To what extent the ideas that were soon to make Campbell the leading figure in the English Palladian movement ultimately derived from Smith is still uncertain, but it seems likely that the association between the two architects was much closer than Campbell was prepared to admit.

Although a good deal of information about Alexander McGill has come to light within recent years he is still rather a shadowy figure. Like Alexander Edward he was the son of an Angus minister, and it was as 'Mr. Alexander M'Gill' (a designation reserved for graduates and others of superior status) that he was apprenticed in 1697 to Alexander Nisbett, a prominent Edinburgh master-mason who had earlier undertaken important contracts in Angus at Panmure House and Glamis Castle. In 1710 McGill was admitted to the Edinburgh masons' lodge *gratis* as an 'architector', and ten years later he was appointed City Architect of Edinburgh, a newly-

54 Design drawing for Melville House, Fife

constituted post which he retained until his death in 1734. McGill's association with James Smith began at least as early as 1709, when the two jointly submitted plans to the Earl of Findlater for remodelling Cullen House (unexecuted), and the partnership evidently continued up to the time of Smith's death, for in 1727 he appears as Smith's assignee in a lawsuit brought against the Earl of Leven for non-payment of sums due for the building of Melville House, while in the same year McGill witnessed an agreement relating to a steam pumping-engine which Smith had installed in his ill-fated coal-mine.

To judge from the major buildings for which he was personally responsible McGill was content to work in the idiom already established by Bruce and Smith. He evidently had a strong feeling for mass, as well as a fascination for grandiose courtyard-layouts of a complexity well beyond the needs, and often also the means, of all but his richest clients. McGill's first large commission was probably Blair Drummond (for George Drummond, 1715–7, demolished 1870), where the main house, a plain hip-roofed block with regular fenestration, was flanked by no less than six separate courts, the outermost one being approached through a convex screen-wall. While work was still going on at Blair Drummond the 2nd Earl of Bute asked McGill to prepare drawings for a large house at Mountstuart (1716–22, main block replaced in the 1740s and again in 1879) on a fine site overlooking the Firth of Clyde. Taking full advantage of the ground the architect produced an interesting scheme incorporating a low two-storeyed front with a recessed centre on the courtyard side, and a three-storeyed elevation, very similar to those of Blair Drummond, overlooking the gardens at the rear, the uppermost floor on this side being entirely taken up by a gallery. In 1717 McGill designed an addition to the Duke of Montrose's Glasgow town house (not completed, demolished c. 1855), giving the principal elevation a balustraded parapet and platform roof as well as rusticated facework reminiscent of that at Yester, but at Donibristle (for the 6th Earl of Moray 1719–23, main block destroyed 1859) he produced a more conservative design incorporating a substantial H-plan block, in part of earlier date, together with an elaborate forecourt layout on two levels, the approach being made by means of a handsome terraced staircase enriched with wrought ironwork.

As well as including leading figures like Edward, Smith and McGill, Bruce's circle also contained several able practitioners drawn from the ranks both of the aristocracy and the master craftsmen. Among the former was Patrick, Ist Earl of Strathmore (1643–95), who when remodelling his castles of Glamis and Lyon (now called Castle Huntly) undertook almost the whole planning and direction of the work himself, disarming professional criticism by the claim that he 'never Judged anything of my owne small endeavours worthie to make so much noice as to call for or invit to either of my houses publick Architecturs'. The Earl of Mar, on the other hand, although himself a designer of no mean ability, went out of his way to cultivate the acquaintance of professional architects such as Alexander Edward, William Adam and James Gibbs, with the last of whom he enjoyed a close working relationship until his death. Lord Mar made extensive improvements to his own estate at Alloa, whose house and gardens, the latter apparently incorporating at least 32 different vistas as well as much fine statuary, greatly impressed early travellers such as Macky and Defoe. After losing estates and title by forfeiture following his part in the Jacobite rebellion of 1715 Mar continued his architectural studies in exile, not only making numerous designs, mainly of a baroque character, for the houses of friends at home and abroad, but also drawing up schemes both for bridging the North Loch, Edinburgh, preparatory to the building of a New Town and for the construction of a canal between the Forth and Clyde estuaries.

Several of the most prominent mason-architects operated within family partnerships, some of which flourished for several generations. Robert Mylne's role as Bruce's principal master-mason during the 1670s has already been mentioned, but he also undertook a good deal of work on his own account, including a single-arched bridge over the Upper Clyde near Abington (1682, demolished c. 1770) and a considerable amount of speculative building in Edinburgh and Leith. The son of a notable sculptor and descendant of a distinguished line of royal master-masons, Robert Mylne himself held the post of master-mason to the Crown until his death in 1710, when he was succeeded in the family business by his son William; his most famous descendant, however, was his grandson Robert (1737–1811), the architect and engineer. Mylne was succeeded as Bruce's master-mason by Tobias Bachop of Alloa, who also did a good deal of government work, principally at Stirling Castle, and was likewise associated with building-operations at Logie Church, Stirlingshire, Panmure House, Cortachy Castle and elsewhere. Bachop was clearly an influential figure in the dissemination of Bruce's version of classicism, for as well as acting as a mason-contractor he also appears to have furnished designs for buildings, including Dumfries Town House (p. 102) and his own dwelling-house in Alloa. The family enterprise in which he played the leading part also included his son Charles and other relatives.

Post-Reformation Churches

The introduction of the Reformed pattern of worship in the third quarter of the sixteenth century brought about a number of important changes of architectural usage. The compartmentation of medieval churches was condemned by the Reformers, to whom the customary divisions of nave, chancel, transept and chapel were so many obstacles to the observance of fully congregational worship. Their principal requirement was a single-chambered building in which people could freely hear the preaching of the Word and take part in the celebration of the Lord's Supper, the congregation being accommodated for this purpose at long communion tables placed within the body of the church. The only major subdivision of the building was of social rather than liturgical significance, the laird and his family, as also the burgh magistrates, invariably preferring to be seated within their own private pews or galleries. These 'lairds' lofts' were frequently placed above a family burial-vault, the whole structure thus forming a separate appendage to the church. Sometimes, as in the sumptuously appointed Hopetoun Aisle (1707–8) at Abercorn, designed by Sir William Bruce, the loft incorporated a comfortable retiring-room in which meals could be taken in the intervals between services.

Of the new churches erected during the first century and a half after the Reformation a large number were of the simple oblong type that had become customary during the later Middle Ages. Stylistically, too, many followed medieval precedents, Gothic forms persisting even more noticeably in the ecclesiastical than in the domestic architecture of the period. The attractive little Tweedside church of Lyne, erected by Lord Hay of Yester in 1640–5, is a fairly representative example of its class. The building is lit by a series of heavily-traceried Gothic windows, the single entrance-doorway being placed towards the west end of the south wall. Lord Yester's original canopied pew survives, together with a contemporary oak pulpit. Less typical of the period, but of greater architectural interest, are two other rectangular kirks, the Chapel Royal at Stirling Castle and the parish church of Dairsie. The former, which was hastily erected for the baptismal ceremonies of Prince Henry in 1594, has a remarkable south elevation in which two-light semicircular-headed windows are symmetrically disposed about a central doorway framed within a rather clumsy classical frontispiece. The internal arrangements have been altered, but some well-preserved early seventeenth-century decoration by the English painter, Valentine Jenkyn, survives. Dairsie was built by Archbishop Spottiswoode in 1621, and its original internal layout, which included a choir-screen, probably reflects current attempts to introduce Anglican liturgical practices into Scotland. The external elevations are a strange mixture of styles in which Renaissance, Scottish Baronial and debased Gothic elements all find a place.

A natural development of the simple rectangle produced the equally characteristic T-plan, in which the projecting wing or 'aisle' frequently housed the laird's burial-vault and loft. Two seventeenth-century Fife churches, Anstruther Easter (1634) and Tulliallan (1675), may serve to illustrate this type. In the former the aisle is quite small, but at Tulliallan it is of the same width as the main body of the church, access to a gallery having been obtained by means of a forestair rising against the east wall. Both churches have western towers, that at Anstruther being little more than a belfry, while the one at Tulliallan, like its neighbour at Airth, on the opposite side of the Forth, is a full-scale structure of some architectural refinement. One of the most ambitious T-plan churches of the period was the Tron Kirk, Edinburgh, begun in 1637 to a design of John Mylne, the King's Master-Mason. The plan is now incomplete, for when the building was

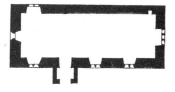

55 Lyne Church,
Peeblesshire: plan

altered and truncated in the late eighteenth century the original south aisle was entirely removed. The steeple, too, has been renewed, but a good deal of original architectural detail survives, some of it reflecting the current Anglo-Flemish Mannerist style and some being of late Gothic character.

Centrally-planned churches were few and far between, the earliest of them being Burntisland, built at the expense of the local inhabitants in 1592. The building is almost square on plan and is surmounted by a central tower carried on semicircular arches springing from rectangular piers, additional support being provided by heavily-buttressed diagonal arches. Most such churches were cruciform, however, the majority being of Greek-cross plan. One of the best preserved is Lauder (1673), designed by Sir William Bruce for the Duke of Lauderdale, who stipulated only that the building should be 'decent and large enough, with a handsom litle steeple'. In the original

56 Canongate Church, Edinburgh

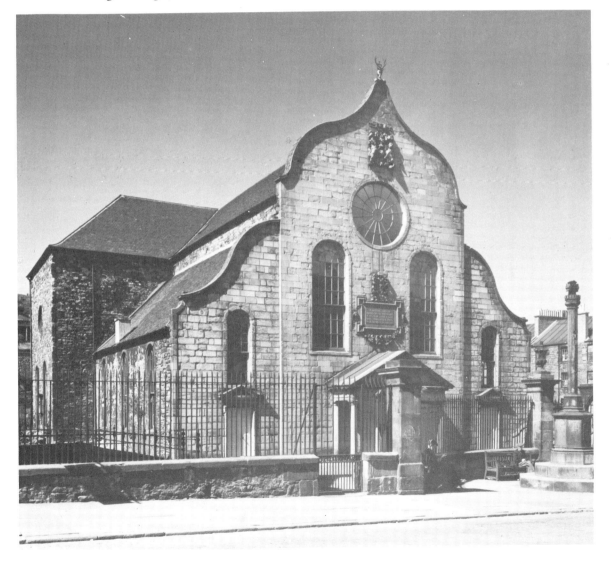

arrangement two at least of the four arms contained lofts, while the eastern one accommodated an altar. Apart from its distinctive plan Bruce's design is firmly set within the vernacular tradition, but the aisled Latin-cross church of the Canongate, Edinburgh, designed and built by James Smith in 1688–90 at a cost of more than £2000 is much more ambitious in character. Its basilican plan, more reminiscent of Continental Catholicism than of

57 Donibristle Chapel, Fife

Scottish Presbyterianism, was evidently fixed upon shortly before the abdication of James II, for whom Smith was concurrently refurnishing the Chapel Royal at Holyroodhouse at great expense for the celebration of the Roman rite. Although the chapel furnishings were subsequently burnt by the Edinburgh mob, the construction of the Canongate church proceeded without serious interruption, the interior being hastily adapted for Reformed worship and Dutch William's coat of arms (apparently carved by Smith himself) prominently displayed upon the south gable.

Smith may also have been responsible for the handsome T-plan kirk at Gifford (1710), where he and Alexander McGill were then engaged in building Yester House. The design is markedly conservative, the tower in particular being almost medieval in spirit, and when McGill reproduced it at Newbattle in 1727 he was careful to update the tower and give the main building a hipped roof. More interesting than either of these, however, are the churches at Mountstuart (1722) and Donibristle (1729–32), both apparently by McGill. Mountstuart is a T-plan building with a swept hipped roof which gives way at each end of the main block to a pedimented gable surmounted by an ogee-roofed bellcot. The ridges of the roof are decorated with scalloped leadwork of the kind familiar from both Smith's and McGill's drawings, while the double-lancet windows are set somewhat uncomfortably within rusticated surrounds. At the small private chapel of Donibristle, however, all such awkwardnesses are overcome and the result is a harmonious Gibbsian composition in miniature, complete with pedimented roof and elegant octagonal belfry.

The early classical period saw the erection of many notable funerary monuments both of foreign and native manufacture. The influence of imported English products like the Dunbar monument (p. 70) is clearly seen in works such as the Menzies monument at Weem (1616) and the Bruce monument at Culross (c. 1642, the figures probably of English workmanship), while a similar development can be traced in the churchyard memorials at Greyfriars, Edinburgh, where the Byres monument, executed by William Wallace in 1629, marks the successful integration of the new style with an arched altar-tomb of traditional form. By the end of the seventeenth century Scottish architects and craftsmen were themselves producing work of very high quality, including such outstanding examples as the fine baroque monument (1696) to the 3rd Duke of Hamilton, designed by James Smith to stand in the church at Hamilton, but later removed to Bothwell, and Alexander Edward's no less exuberant memorial (c. 1703) to the Marquess of Atholl at Dunkeld Cathedral, with its elaborate display of family genealogy and heraldry. But the most remarkable church monuments of the period are undoubtedly the 'Queensberry Marbles' at Durisdeer. Here, within a remote and unpretentious country kirk there may be seen the vast baldacchino of white marble that was erected over the burial-vault of the 1st Duke of Queensberry, the builder of Drumlanrig Castle, to a design of James Smith in 1695–1708, and beside it the more orthodox mural

58 Queensberry
Monument, Durisdeer
Church, Dumfriesshire

monument to the 2nd Duke, carved by the celebrated Anglo-Dutch sculptor
John Van Nost in 1713 at a cost of £400.

Burghs

Contrary to popular belief few if any buildings of medieval date, apart from
a handful of churches, now survive in Scottish towns. Nor as yet do we have
more than a very rough idea of what early burgh dwellings looked like,
although timber, wattle-and-daub and thatch, rather than stone and slate,

should probably be visualized as the standard building materials. It is to be hoped that archaeological excavation, now at last beginning to respond to the widespread opportunities for investigation currently provided by urban redevelopment, will considerably extend our knowledge of this subject within the next two or three decades.

But even when buildings disappear streets usually remain, and many early Scottish burghs still in this way retain clear traces of their original street-plans. A common layout, seen for example at Edinburgh, Jedburgh and Forres, comprised a single main street running like a backbone from the gates of the royal or baronial castle beneath whose protective walls the community had first been established to a gateway situated at the opposite end of the burgh. This axial street, usually known as High Street, was utilized both as a thoroughfare and market-place, and from it blocks of buildings served by lesser streets and closes led off at right angles. By the later Middle Ages, if not before, many of the more important burghs were enclosed by defensive walls of stone, and considerable stretches of these still survive in Edinburgh, Stirling, Peebles and Haddington, together with a single fortified gateway, namely the West Port, St Andrews, built by a local mason in 1589.

Up to about the second half of the seventeenth century most houses in Scottish towns seem to have been built mainly of timber with thatched roofs. Writing in 1656 the English traveller Richard Franck noted that the buildings of Aberdeen were 'framed with stone and timber', while a French traveller who visited Glasgow a few years later reported that 'the houses are only of wood, ornamented with carving'. Even in Edinburgh, where stone was more widely used, it was not until 1674 that the town council ordained that all new buildings were to be constructed of this material, and five years later the Scottish parliament found it necessary to renew legislation requiring heritors of thatched houses to replace the thatch with lead, slates or tiles within a year.

Some houses were self-contained, but flatted buildings several storeys in height became increasingly common in the more prosperous towns, where shortage of space made vertical expansion a necessity. Thus there evolved the tall tenement buildings that remain one of the most characteristic features of the Scottish burgh – though vertical living can hardly have come as a novelty to a nation whose upper classes had for so long resided in tower-houses. Standards of accommodation varied widely, but the well-to-do Edinburgh merchant of the early seventeenth century would have reckoned himself comfortably housed if he had a hall and kitchen, three or four chambers, a gallery and one or more cellars; if he lived on one of the upper floors of the building, part of the ascent would be made by means of a stone forestair rising directly from the street.

One of the last part-timbered buildings to survive in a Scottish burgh was the Kinnoull Lodging, Perth, built for George Hay, later 1st Earl of Kinnoull, in about 1600 and demolished only in 1968. The main fabric of

59 West Port, St
Andrews, Fife

this three-storeyed building was of stone, as was also the projecting circular
staircase, but the street frontage also incorporated an overhanging gallery
of timber box-frame construction. One or two restored or reconstructed
buildings of this type are still extant, including 'John Knox's House' and
Huntly House, Edinburgh, while corbelled frontages of stone which echo
timber prototypes can be seen at Moray House, Edinburgh, and Sailors'
Walk, Kirkcaldy. In the same way timber posts carrying the front upper
portion of a house over a pedestrian thoroughfare were translated into
stone columns, thus producing the arcaded fronts so characteristic of late
seventeenth-century burgh architecture, and of which examples still survive
in Edinburgh and Elgin.

The pace of transition from timber to stone construction varied a good
deal from place to place, but nowhere were more substantial stone-built
houses erected in the later sixteenth and seventeenth centuries than in the

thriving seaport burghs of Fife. At this period the development of coastal shipping and the growth of trade with Low Country and Baltic ports brought great prosperity to an area naturally endowed with almost unlimited supplies of excellent freestone. Thus, as burgh after burgh obtained its formal charter of privileges – no less than five towns on the south coast were erected into royal burghs between 1541 and 1588 – so was each dignified by handsome new houses constructed for wealthy merchants and sea-captains.

The best preserved of these burghs is Culross, which retains many of its original cobbled causeways and numerous two- and three-storeyed houses built of harled rubble masonry with dressings of yellow sandstone and roofed with red pantile, a type of covering widely used throughout central and eastern Scotland during the seventeenth and eighteenth centuries. Some of the houses are flatted, the upper floors being reached by means of open forestairs, and many display carved embellishments such as ornate dormer-window pediments, trade symbols, 'date-stones' and pious inscriptions.

Among the historic burghs of central Scotland, Linlithgow and Clackmannan have lost most of their early buildings but retain their street-plans, while Stirling retains both its medieval street-plan and a sprinkling of much-restored buildings of late sixteenth- and seventeenth-century date, the best of these being Town-Clerk Norrie's house (1671) in Broad Street, which has an ashlar frontage enriched with pilasters and inscribed window-pediments. Further north both Stonehaven and Inverness contain a few buildings of this period, but nothing to compare with the fine series of burgh houses to be found at Kirkwall, in Orkney, where regional characteristics are also well marked, most buildings being constructed of local flagstone laid in clay mortar and roofed with heavy stone slates.

Although burgh houses were usually closely packed, often presenting no more than a gable end to the street, many of the larger towns also contained a number of more substantial detached residences belonging either to the nobility or to rich merchants. So far as the comparatively restricted nature of an urban site allowed these buildings were generally similar in character to those erected by the upper classes upon their country estates, a courtyard layout frequently being favoured for the largest houses and a tower-house plan for the remainder.

A good example of the former type is the 'great ludging' erected by the Dowager Countess of Home in the Edinburgh Canongate in about the third decade of the seventeenth century under the direction of the King's Master-Mason, William Wallace. Moray House, as the building has been called since 1643, was originally quadrangular on plan, the extensive grounds to the south being laid out as gardens and orchards, but only the north and west sides of the early house now remain. The Anglo-Flemish detail and the tall diagonally-set chimneys recall Wallace's work at Linlithgow Palace and Heriot's Hospital, while the rich Jacobean plasterwork that is such a notable feature of the interiors is a no less typical ingredient of the current

60 Tanhouse Brae and
The Study, Culross, Fife

Scottish Renaissance style. Close by is Lord Hatton's Lodging (c. 1680, now called Queensberry House), probably designed by James Smith, a dignified half-H-plan building which likewise at one time contained much fine interior decoration.

Although Edinburgh successfully established her claim to be the Scottish capital by the reign of James IV, Stirling remained a favourite seat of the Court for another century before declining into what John Ray described, somewhat patronisingly, as 'an indifferently handsome town' having 'a good market-place and two palaces'. Of the two buildings thus referred to in 1662 the first, Mar's Work, is a structure of exceptional interest, built during the most violent years of Mary Queen of Scots' reign as the private residence of a great nobleman who was shortly to become Regent of Scotland. The plan adopted makes little concession to the urban environment, being in all respects similar to that of a contemporary courtyard-castle such as Tolquhon. The building was never finished and only the east range of the courtyard now survives, its octagonal-towered gatehouse and gun-looped basement fronting the main approach to Stirling Castle. The principal façade is of regular design but much overlaid by heraldic carving and other ornamental sculpture, some of it evidently copied from James V's nearby palace at the castle.

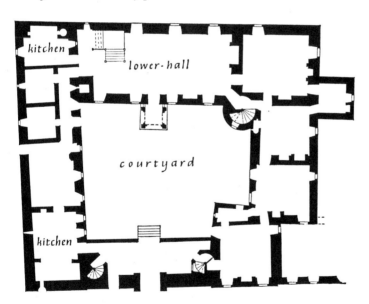

61 Argyll Lodging, Stirling: plan

The second house that caught Ray's eye as he made his way up to the castle, Argyll Lodging, ranks as the finest surviving example of its class in the country. Its principal creator, William Alexander, Viscount Stirling, was one of the most colourful figures at Charles I's court; poet, scholar, statesman and adventurer, he succeeded in making himself one of the best known, if least loved, men of his day only to have his career shattered in mid course by financial ruin. Alexander remodelled and enlarged an existing building on the site to form two ranges of a quadrangular house and part of a third range; the plan was completed by the Earl of Argyll in 1674, the courtyard being closed on the remaining side by a handsome screen-wall containing an entrance-gateway. There is a very generous provision of accommodation and it is noticeable that a number of the principal apartments, instead of occupying their customary position above a vaulted cellarage, are disposed at ground-floor level, an arrangement which marked a decisive step forward in planning. The courtyard elevations are elaborately decorated in the Scottish Renaissance style, suggesting the hand of William Ayton or some other follower of William Wallace.

The tower-house type of house is well illustrated by 'Wallace's Tower', Aberdeen, recently removed from its original site in Nether Kirkgate and re-erected in another part of the city. This tall Z-plan building (c. 1600) makes no attempt to disguise its affinities with contemporary Aberdeenshire castles, such as Terpersie and Pitcaple, although specifically defensive features are absent. Other good examples of similar date are the Kellie Lodging, Pittenweem, and the former residence of the Earls of Cassillis at Maybole, this last being a modest L-plan tower-house incorporating distinctive carved detail of a type found in a closely-related group of contemporary Ayrshire and Galloway castles. Sir Thomas MacLellan of Bombie, a one-time provost of Kirkcudbright, also provided himself with a town residence of unusual splendour, taking as his model one of the more substantial tower-houses of the day, such as Elcho Castle, in which castellated and domestic features are found in combination. The plan is basically L-shaped, with an extruded staircase in the re-entrant angle and an additional corner-tower, but apart from the provision of gun-ports little care has been taken to make the building defensible.

After the parish church the two most important buildings in any Scottish burgh were the market-cross and the tolbooth. The cross, as the essential symbol of burghal status, always occupied a prominent position in the main street or market place. Here formal proclamations of local and national import were made, criminals were punished and, on occasions of public rejoicing, there was festivity and banqueting. The earliest market-crosses were probably of timber, but all the surviving examples are of stone except that at Kilwinning, which retains a wooden cross-head. Cruciform examples of any description are, in fact, rare, the shaft usually rising to a decorative capital bearing a coat of arms or a sundial, and often surmounted by a unicorn or other finial. In most cases the cross is set upon a stepped base, but a number stand upon stone platforms of some architectural elaboration, one of the finest of these being that at Prestonpans, which dates from the early seventeenth century.

At the tolbooth, or Town House (as it latterly came to be called), the public affairs of the burgh were transacted and criminals imprisoned. For reasons both of prestige and security the earlier tolbooths, such as Tain, followed the familiar tower-house pattern, a belfry usually being added to

62 Crail Tolbooth, Fife

carry the town bell. By themselves towers such as these could provide only a very limited amount of accommodation, however, and when more spacious rooms came to be required the obvious solution was to extend the building horizontally, as at Edinburgh Canongate and Musselburgh, where a new tolbooth was erected in about 1590 in the form of a long open-parapeted block with a tower at one end. Most of the larger seventeenth-century tolbooths seem to have been provided with prominent steeples, and a particularly handsome specimen in the Scottish Renaissance style may still be seen in Glasgow, although the tolbooth itself has long since disappeared.

During the second half of the seventeenth century buildings of more formal character began to appear, one of the earliest being Linlithgow

Tolbooth, designed by a local master-mason in 1668. The thorough-going restoration carried out nearly 200 years later makes it hard to determine the original appearance of this building, but it seems to have been an oblong three-storeyed block of simple classical style with a tall square tower projecting from the centre of the rear elevation, the whole well lit by means of regularly-spaced windows having flat triangular-headed pediments with enriched tympana. When the opportunity to erect a new Town House in Stirling came in 1702, however, the council commissioned a plan from Sir William Bruce, who designed a compact but elegant building having a carefully-detailed ashlar front (subsequently lengthened by three bays) and a fine six-storeyed spire which takes full advantage of its corner site. Bruce's design was closely followed by Tobias Bachop in his scheme for Dumfries Town House (the Midsteeple) a year or two later.

4
Georgian Achievement

Although the Act of Union and the Hanoverian succession ushered in an era of comparative stability, Scotland for long remained an underdeveloped country, her closer ties with England serving only to emphasize the backwardness of her own economy. These were scarcely the conditions in which architecture could be expected to flourish, and despite Ramsay of Ochtertyre's claim that 'after the Union ... our country gentlemen began to show some inclination for better houses' few private or public buildings of the first rank were erected before the third quarter of the eighteenth century, while the two most able Scottish architects of the period, Colin Campbell and James Gibbs, had to look to England for their opportunities. Soon after the accession of George III, however, the tide began to turn and before the end of the century a general improvement in trade, coupled with rapid developments both in industry and agriculture, brought Scotland at last to the threshold of prosperity. These factors soon led to an upsurge in building activity, at first manifested mainly in the coastal burghs and on the estates of the lowland gentry, but ultimately penetrating to most parts of the country and affecting all ranks of society.

William Adam and Sons
The dominant figure in Scottish architecture during the period between the Fifteen and the Forty-five was unquestionably William Adam, the son of a Kirkcaldy builder whose forebears had long been established as small lairds in Angus. Enterprising and ambitious, and possessing a shrewd head for business as well as considerable artistic ability, Adam rose rapidly to distinction, although this would scarcely have been possible had his engaging manner not won him patrons such as the 2nd Earl of Stair and Sir John Clerk, who gave him entrée to the leading political and intellectual circles of the day. In 1728 Adam was made a burgess of Edinburgh for services rendered to the burgh, while in the same year he obtained the government post of Clerk and Storekeeper of the Works, to be followed in 1730 by the more important appointment of Mason to the Board of Ordnance in North Britain. Nor did he neglect private business-interests, projects for brick and coal works, salt-pans, mills, canals and aqueducts all flourishing under his direction, and the ensuing profits being invested partly in Edinburgh house property and partly in the purchase of a small estate on

the borders of Fife and Kinross-shire, which he promptly renamed Blair Adam. Early in his career Adam conceived the idea of publishing a volume of engravings illustrative of his own and of other leading Scottish architects' works, and many of his designs were engraved on a subscription basis with this end in view. The project was unrealised at the time of Adam's death in 1748, however, and it was not until about 1812 that an enlarged edition of the book was published by his grandson under the somewhat grandiose title of *Vitruvius Scoticus*. A more important legacy was the family business itself, in which the eldest of Adam's four sons, John, had already begun to play an active part, for it was from this closely knit circle that the 'promising young men' (as the writer of one of their father's obituary notices termed them) were ultimately to go out to carry the name of Adam throughout western Europe and into the New World.

Looking through the pages of *Vitruvius Scoticus* it is hard to distinguish any coherent architectural style in William Adam's designs; indeed his work is remarkable as much for its eclecticism as for its unevenness of quality. His indebtedness to Gibbs and Vanbrugh is manifest, while Dutch and French sources seem also to have been laid under tribute from time to time. For the severities of English Palladianism, on the other hand, Adam evidently had little taste, although he could when called upon – as for example at Newliston and Haddo – express himself convincingly enough in that idiom. Despite the fact that many of his designs appear bizarre or ungainly, some of his work achieved real dignity and grandeur, hardly any was dull, and all of it displayed a robustness and directness of expression entirely appropriate to the artistic climate of North Britain.

Little is known of Adam's training and early professional career, his first recorded architectural activities dating from the early 1720s, when he was already more than 30 years of age. One of his earliest known commissions came from Sir John Clerk, who called him in to assist in the construction of a small country house at Mavisbank, an attractive property lying about halfway between Edinburgh and the family's principal residence at Penicuik. Few classical houses of such modest size had hitherto been erected in Scotland and the main features of the scheme were conceived by Sir John himself, who may have been influenced by James Smith's designs for New Hailes and Raith and by Colin Campbell's pioneering essay at Shawfield, Glasgow (1712, demolished). Nevertheless, as completed in about 1727 Mavisbank was as much of a novelty as Dunkeld had been half a century earlier and little less influential; a free translation of a Palladian villa, elegant in appearance and compact of plan, Sir John's house at once set a new fashion for Scottish country mansions of lesser rank. Indeed, before Mavisbank was finished Adam had already begun to build a second house of similar type nearby for Lord Somerville and his wife, who during a recent period of residence in Wiltshire may perhaps have had the opportunity of seeing Henry Hoare's newly completed villa at Stourhead. Here at Drum, away from the restraining influence of Sir John Clerk, the architect made even bolder use of surface decoration, crowding the principal façade with a rich assortment of Palladian and Gibbsian motifs and allowing his stuccoer, Samuel Calderwood, free rein within. Apart from the fact that the house embodies an unusually spacious oval staircase, the plan of Drum is conventional enough. For the villa he designed for the 2nd Duke of Atholl at Tullibardine, however, Adam adopted a markedly Palladian layout incorporating a main block 68 feet square with a central top-lit staircase and several correctly proportioned rooms; but this was never built.

Another interesting house of compact form that probably reflects the influence of the Anglo-Palladian villa is Dun, erected for David Erskine, Lord Dun, in 1730. The most distinctive feature of the design is the 'triumphal arch' centrepiece of the principal elevation which strikes a distinctly Vanbrughian note, although the idea in this case seems to be derived from a somewhat earlier scheme for Dun conceived by the Earl of Mar. The stuccowork is similar in character to that at Drum. Finally among

63 Dun House, Angus. Saloon

Adam's villas mention should be made of Lord Minto's Edinburgh town house (c. 1739, demolished) and Hamilton Hall, Midlothian (1745, demolished), where the architect in each case achieved considerable refinement of design within a remarkably small compass.

Although most of Adam's mansions were of fairly modest size, he twice had the opportunity to build on a grand scale. Early in the 1720s the 1st Earl of Hopetoun gave the architect the task of remodelling and enlarging the mansion that Sir William Bruce had completed for him only twenty years previously (p. 80), and as the Earl's ideas took shape it became clear that he intended to create a house of a size and splendour hitherto unknown in Scotland. Adam's design for the principal elevation seems to be indebted in varying degrees both to Wren and Vanbrugh, the ponderous attic storey, scarcely interrupted by the pediment of the great tetrastyle portico that was intended to provide a centrepiece, looking back to Hampton Court and the giant order of Corinthian pilasters, the emphatic round-headed windows and the curved return-bays no less strongly recalling Castle Howard. Both patron and architect died before the project was completed and in 1750 the 2nd Earl, in an endeavour to bring matters to a speedy conclusion, allowed John and Robert Adam to revise the design in several particulars, notably by the omission of the central portico and its associated double staircase. This removed the focus of the whole composition, accentuated the massiveness of the central block and threatened dullness – an effect skilfully countered by the introduction of a new note of lightness in a modified design for the pavilions.

William Adam's second chance to build a country mansion of the first rank came in 1730, when William Duff (later Baron Braco and Earl of Fife), a wealthy Whig landowner, commissioned him to erect a suitably imposing house on his Banffshire estates. Both in plan and massing the central unit, comprising a tall oblong block with square angle-towers linked by quadrant walls to pavilions, recalls Vanbrugh's designs for Eastbury, published five years earlier in the third volume of *Vitruvius Britannicus*, but there is little doubt that Adam's own Hopetoun drawings provided the immediate source of inspiration for the elevations. Although the pavilions and screens were never built Duff House is undoubtedly the most arresting of all the architect's surviving works; a medieval castle in baroque dress its rich texture and towering bulk convey a memorable impression of seignorial pomp.

In addition to his country houses Adam designed a number of public buildings in Edinburgh and elsewhere, of which the Edinburgh Royal Infirmary (1738, demolished), with its elaborate domed centrepiece, was the most imposing and College Library, Glasgow (1732, demolished), a manifestly Gibbsian composition, the most elegant. He also enjoyed a considerable reputation as a garden designer, most of his layouts being conventional essays in the formal manner of Wise or Bridgeman, although at Arniston (1726, for Robert Dundas) he introduced a number of

naturalistic features which probably reflect the ideas of his friend Sir John   64 Duff House, Banff
Clerk. Adam's most remarkable piece of garden design, however, the retreat
and hunting-lodge erected for the 5th Duke of Hamilton at Chatelherault in
1732, seems to have been very much a product of his own creation. Designed
to serve both as a terminal feature to the main south vista from Hamilton
Palace and as the frontispiece to a walled flower-garden, the composition is
one of great boldness and originality.

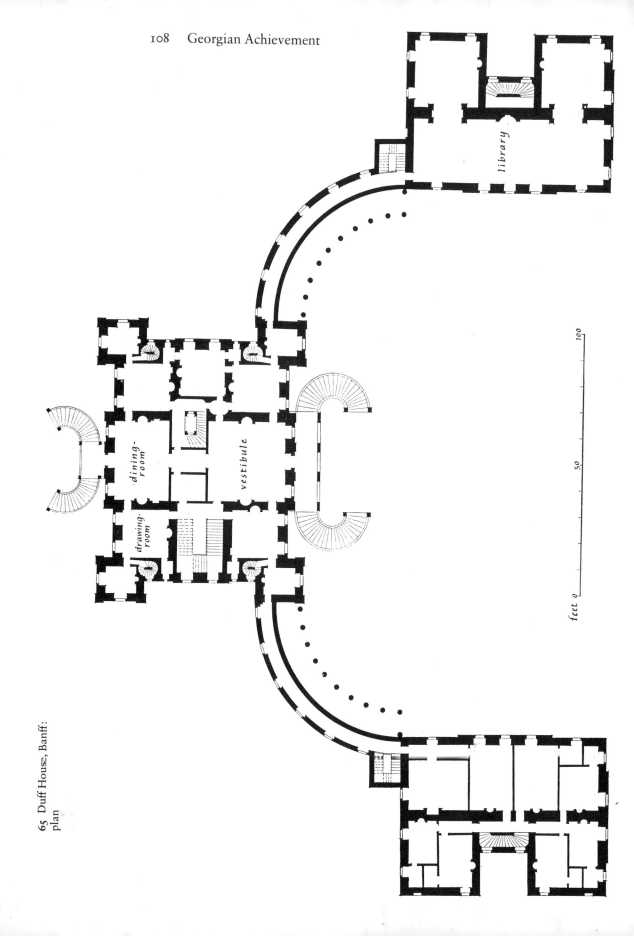

library

dining-room

vestibule

drawing-room

feet 0   50   100

65 Duff House, Banff:
plan

Following William Adam's death in 1748 the family business was taken over by his two eldest sons, John and Robert, who had already gained a certain amount of architectural experience through assisting their father in some of his more important projects. The third son, James, did not formally join the partnership until his return from Italy in 1763, although his early sketchbooks contain a number of drawings, including one for Gunsgreen House, Eyemouth (c. 1755), which suggest that he was already active as a designer at this period. With Robert spending much of the 1750s touring the Continent under the patronage of the Hope family, the conduct of affairs at first fell mainly to the senior partner, John, who although less gifted than either Robert or James possessed both architectural competence and business acumen in good measure. Indeed, it was not the least of his achievements to establish the partnership upon a basis sound enough to warrant the firm's subsequent transfer to London.

Almost as if in protest against his father's exuberant stylistic eclecticism John Adam showed a consistent preference for a restrained brand of English Palladianism, and apart from the neo-Gothic Douglas Castle (p. 120) nearly all his work was executed in this idiom. His rather formal manner is seen to advantage at Dumfries House, Ayrshire, erected for the 4th Earl of Dumfries in 1754–9, while the old-fashioned dignity of Moffat House (for the 2nd Earl of Hopetoun, 1762), with its tall main block and bell-cast roofs, is enlivened only by the beautifully contrasted texture of the masonry.

66 Dumfries House, Ayrshire

When occasion demanded, however, Adam could produce designs of considerable originality, and the little villa that he built at Hawkhill, near Edinburgh (1757, demolished), as a suburban retreat for the Solicitor-General, Andrew Pringle of Haining, contained an ingeniously planned 'piano nobile' complete with two well-proportioned and richly decorated public rooms. His two most important public buildings, both markedly conservative in design, were Inveraray Town House (1755–7) and the Edinburgh Exchange (1753–61, now City Chambers), this last following the customary courtyard plan, with a piazza on one side for the transaction of business.

The dominance of the Adam family left little room for other contenders, unless possessed of independent status or established reputation. Prominent among the former were the Clerks of Penicuik, who produced three gentlemen architects in successive generations, the most notable of these being William Adam's patron and mentor, Sir John Clerk, 2nd Baronet. A respected member of leading English Palladian circles and friend of Lords Burlington and Pembroke, Sir John occupied a prominent position in lowland society and soon came to be regarded as an arbiter of taste in all matters relating to architecture and landscape gardening. He exercised his influence mainly through advice and patronage, a well-attested example of his intervention occurring at Haddo House (1732–5), where Lord Aberdeen allowed him to modify William Adam's design in order to achieve a more restrained effect. Penicuik House itself (1761–9, gutted by fire), an uncompromising essay in English Palladianism, was designed not by Sir John, but by his son and successor, Sir James Clerk, who was also responsible for the correct little classical church (1771) in the neighbouring burgh of Penicuik.

The execution of several of the Clerk family's more important projects, including Mavisbank and Penicuik House itself, was entrusted to John Baxter, an Edinburgh mason of considerable ability both as craftsman and designer. With Sir John's help Baxter soon established himself as an architect in his own right, his most important commission probably being Galloway House (for Lord Garlies, c. 1740), where he based his design upon a scheme previously submitted by John Douglas. Not surprisingly, the house as built shows Baxter to have been well versed in the Palladian ideas of his patron, but his handling of the pedimented centrepiece of the main block displays a certain provincial clumsiness.

Most of the other Scottish architects of the period are still rather shadowy figures, but it is doubtful if future research will do much to enhance their reputations. Douglas himself, who practised in Edinburgh, is known to have designed and built several houses in different parts of Scotland. He was described by one contemporary as 'next in character to Mr Adams', but his designs for remodelling Blair Castle (for the 2nd Duke of Atholl, 1736, unexecuted) are insipid, while the very plain three-storeyed block with arcaded ground-floor loggia that he erected along the north side of the quadrangle at St Salvator's College, St Andrews (1754–7), was considered so unsatisfactory that it had to be replaced after less than 80 years. Thomas Mylne, a member of the well-known family of master-masons (p. 89), built a number of houses in and around Edinburgh, the only identifiable one to survive being Inveresk Manor House (1745), an unsophisticated building of conventional classical design. More talented, perhaps, than either of these was Thomas Gibson, known only as the architect of Marchmont House (for the 3rd Earl of Marchmont, 1750–4, remodelled by Lorimer, 1913–6), where he employed the Palladian vocabulary with great assurance and individuality.

Two designers mainly of English reputation also made notable contributions to the early Georgian architecture of Scotland. James Gibbs exerted his influence principally through his books, which were assiduously quarried for ideas by architects and craftsmen alike, his only significant Scottish works being Balvenie House (for William Duff of Braco, 1724, demolished) and St Nicholas West Church, Aberdeen, whose well thought-out plan he provided free of charge to his native city. Isaac Ware, a staunch Palladian, was responsible for two country houses in Scotland, both of villa type, while his designs for a third evidently served as a model for Paxton (for Patrick Home of Billie, 1759–63) which, with its porticoed main block, quadrant walls and trim pavilions stands out as a singularly elegant representation of contemporary English taste.

Church building continued at a modest rate, with but few innovations in design, the majority of rural churches, at least, being plain rectangular or T-plan structures of the plainest description. In the towns, however, there were one or two new developments, such as the appearance of the galleried hall kirk of the type that had already become familiar in England as a result of the work of Wren and Gibbs. Mention has already been made of the latter's design for St Nicholas West (1755), in which he successfully married what was virtually a London city church to a pre-existing Scots Gothic choir and crossing. Gibbs's influence is equally apparent in Allan Dreghorn's almost contemporary church of St Andrew, Glasgow, whose impressive pedimented portico and elegant steeple, no less than the boldly rusticated window architraves, clearly recall St Martin-in-the-Fields.

Centrally-planned churches were always the exception, but several interesting designs were formulated. One of the most ambitious, if least original, is to be found at Hamilton Parish Church (1732), whose academic 'wheel-cross' plan William Adam seems to have borrowed from the fifth book of Serlio's *Architettura*. By utilizing one limb of the building as a portico and vestry, however, and imposing the familiar T-plan arrangement upon the remainder, the architect showed considerable ingenuity in reconciling Renaissance theory with the realities of Presbyterian worship. Adam also wanted to build a circular church at Inveraray, but although this idea was taken over and imaginatively developed by his son John it came to nothing. The most remarkable feature of John Adam's plan, namely the combination under the same roof of separate auditoria serving English- and Gaelic-speaking congregations respectively, was, however, retained in Robert Mylne's final scheme of 1795–1802.

Scottish Neo-Classicism and the Concept of Styles

Although three of the most prominent British architects of the later eighteenth century were Scotsmen, their activities were inevitably centred upon London, and only one of them, Robert Adam, practised extensively in his native land. Adam's most distinctive contribution to Scottish architecture was the series of Georgian Gothic castles described later in this chapter (p. 120), and only two other of his country houses call for mention. The architect's mature classical style is exemplarily expressed at Newliston (for Thomas Hogg, 1789–92), while Gosford (for the 7th Earl of Wemyss, 1792–1800) would surely have ranked as one of his most imposing and assured designs had not the building been altered in execution and soon afterwards shorn of its wings (lavishly rebuilt by William Young, 1883). The three principal rooms in the central block, designed to house the Earl's collection of pictures, rose through two storeys and were to have been surmounted by a low circular dome, the whole composition being conceived on a monumental scale.

Surprisingly enough it was in Scotland too, that Adam found his chief opportunites for monumental design so far as public buildings were concerned. The most successful of these was Register House, Edinburgh, a repository for the public records of Scotland, which was begun in 1774 upon a key site at the intersection of the newly completed South Bridge and Princes Steet. Adam's design, echoing his earlier scheme for Syon House, was for a rotunda within a square courtyard, but the construction of the north range was deferred until the 1820s, being then entrusted to Robert Reid. The elevations are plain but dignified, while the strictly functional plan incorporated such features as counter-opposed vaults and an ingeniously designed central-heating system for the 'Dome'. The commission to undertake the rebuilding of the University of Edinburgh came only a few years before the architect's death, and once again Adam was denied the satisfaction of seeing his scheme brought to full fruition. The design was a bold one which admirably exploited the potential of the site. It embodied two courts of unequal size and differing levels, the lesser forming an atrium to which entrance was gained by means of a monumental portico in the centre of the principal façade. Little of this had been completed by 1793, however, when shortage of funds brought the work to a halt, and it was not until after the Napoleonic Wars that building was recommenced upon a more economical scheme which allowed for only a single court. W. H. Playfair, who won the competition for a revised design, did his best to resolve the resulting problem of levels, but his efforts were not altogether successful, and although he managed to preserve much of the external character of the building none of Adam's interiors were executed. Glasgow,

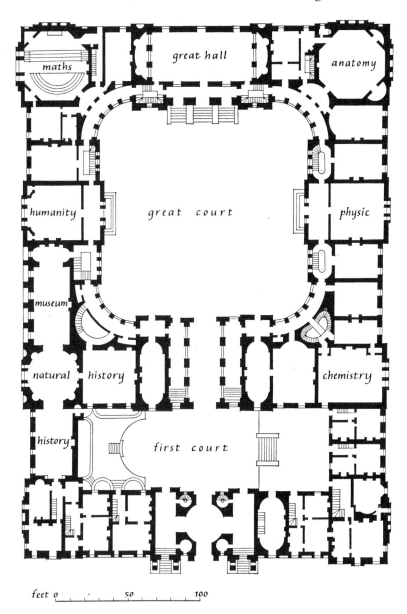

maths

great hall

anatomy

humanity

great court

physic

museum

natural history

chemistry

history

first court

67 Edinburgh University: plan

too, benefited greatly from the genius of Robert and James Adam at this period, but of the three major public buildings that they produced between them during the 1790s only the rather over-designed Trades Hall survives.

Robert Adam's chief rival, Sir William Chambers, was responsible for only one Scottish building of the first rank, although he also built two town houses in St Andrew's Square, Edinburgh. Duddingston House, erected for the bachelor Earl of Abercorn in 1763–8, was a most advanced design which exerted a considerable influence throughout Britain and beyond. Essentially a re-interpretation of the Palladian villa in neo-classical terms the house comprised a square two-storeyed block with a temple portico, the omission

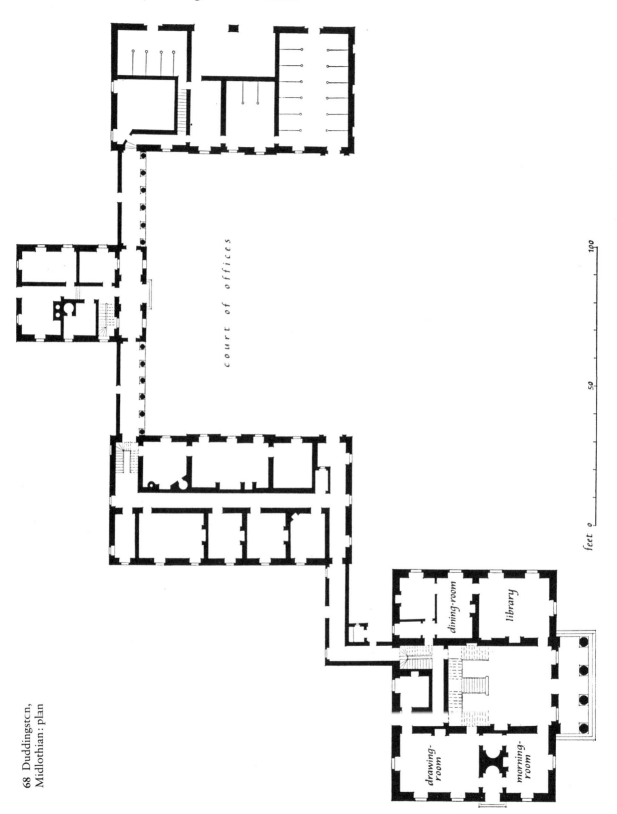

court of offices

dining-room

library

drawing-room

morning-room

68 Duddingstcn,
Midlothian: plan

feet 0   50   100

of the customary basement allowing direct access to the principal floor; kitchens and service quarters were grouped within an adjacent court of offices.

Robert Mylne, third of this trio and the most distinguished member of the Mylne family of architects, designed several houses in Scotland. The most notable of these is Cally (for James Murray of Broughton, 1759–63; alterations and additions by J. B. Papworth, 1833–7), which although of conventional villa plan is given interest by a boldly-contrasted colour scheme in which white Creetown granite is employed in conjunction with dressings of red sandstone. Working in a rather different vein Mylne also played a prominent part in the 5th Duke of Argyll's operations at Inveraray, where he continued the layout of the new town and policies and decorated the principal rooms of the castle in a rich and elegant manner with the aid of English, Scottish and French craftsmen. Earlier in date than any of these, however, is the delightful little St Cecilia's Hall, Edinburgh (1761–3; restored by I. G. Lindsay, 1966), whose elliptically-planned concert room affords both visual and acoustic harmony in equal perfection.

Among other architects of English reputation who practised in Scotland at the turn of the century were Robert Mitchell and Thomas Harrison, but although the former's Preston Hall (for Alexander Callendar, 1791–1800) remains a singularly accomplished example of the fully developed neo-Palladian country house, complete with matching retinue of estate buildings, neither produced a building of any great originality. In the work of the two contemporary Scottish architects, James Playfair and Robert Reid, however, a response can be detected, unmistakeable if at times muted, to the current ideals of Continental neo-classicism.

Playfair's death in 1794 at the age of 39 cut short a career of great promise. The son of an Angus minister, and younger brother of the distinguished mathematician, Playfair established himself as an architect in London in about 1783, receiving considerable support from Henry Dundas, Viscount Melville, for whom he designed the quasi-Gothic Melville Castle (1786). His early classical works, such as Forfar Town Hall (1785) are straightforward enough, but following a visit to France in 1787 he began to produce a number of highly sophisticated designs redolent of the style of Boulée or Ledoux. The massive domed 'Marine Pavilion', linked to a circular court of offices, that he proposed to erect on the shores of Loch Fyne for Sir Alexander Campbell of Ardkinglas (1791) was never realized, but the same bold exploitation of simple geometrical forms can be seen at Cairness (for Charles Gordon, 1789–97), where it was combined with a decidedly eclectic scheme of interior decoration. The courtyard behind the house is semicircular on plan, with a freestanding cylindrical icehouse and remarkable primitivist pavilions on each flank. Most of the interiors are Greek, but there is one notable Egyptian room, perhaps the first in Britain.

Robert Reid, chief government architect in Scotland from 1803–38, played an important role in the development of Georgian Edinburgh, laying

69 Cairness House, Aberdeenshire

out much of the second New Town and designing several major public buildings. Contemporary critics who compared his work unfavourably with that of Robert Adam may seem in retrospect to have missed the point, for while Reid's Adamesque designs, such as the Parliament Square complex, were no doubt undistinguished, some at least of his buildings should be judged rather as early if tentative essays in pursuit of the Greek ideal. This is particularly the case with St George's, Charlotte Square (1811–14, replacing an earlier design by Robert Adam) and Leith Custom House (1811–12), where simple geometric massing is in each case the dominating feature of the composition, while in the picture-gallery at Paxton House Reid created an elegant neo-classical interior incorporating arched exedrae and a central oculus.

It was, of course, in Edinburgh that the architects of the Scottish Greek Revival were to find their greatest opportunities. Already by the end of the century James Craig's simple grid-plan layout (1768) for a New Town on the ridge beyond the North Loch had been found too restricted and building had begun on the eastern and northern approaches. In the initial stages of Craig's project, as it is seen in St Andrew's Square and Queen Street, no strict uniformity of frontage was imposed, but after Robert Adam's successful design for Charlotte Square in 1791 it became usual to treat whole blocks of houses as individual architectural units. In 1815 the line of Princes Street was extended eastwards towards the Calton Hill, a new street, Waterloo Place, being carried across the intervening valley by means of the Regent Bridge. The architect of this project, which in part echoed Nash's design for the approach to Regent Street, London, was Archibald Elliot, who practised jointly with his brother James (d. 1810) from offices in Edinburgh and London. For his Regent Bridge scheme Elliot adopted the Greek style (although his adjacent gaol was castellated) and this was maintained by W. H. Playfair for the terraces that were gradually laid out round the Calton Hill.

Playfair, a younger son of James Playfair, was a pupil of the Glasgow architect William Stark, but also visited France and London, where he is thought to have trained with Robert Smirke. With such a background, together with abundant talents of his own, he found himself singularly well placed to take advantage of the great opportunities afforded by the creation of 'The Modern Athens', and all his best work, with the exception of the powerful but highly idiosyncratic St Stephen's Church (1827), was in the Greek Revival style. For the Calton Hill itself he designed a new and many-porticoed observatory (1818) and two fine monuments, at the same time assuming responsibility for the construction of C. R. Cockerell's ill-fated National Monument, or Parthenon (1822–   ). In the Royal Institution (1823 36, now the Royal Scottish Academy) and the National Gallery (1845–50) Playfair also gave Edinburgh its most familiar pair of Grecian buildings, although neither shows quite the same grasp of composition as the Royal College of Surgeons (1829), where the numerous difficulties presented by the cramped nature of the site were triumphantly resolved.

Rivalling Playfair in his mastery of the Greek style was Thomas Hamilton, the son of an Edinburgh builder, who in 1825 was commissioned by the town council to design a new Royal High School on a commanding site on the south side of the Calton Hill, overlooking the burgh of the Canongate. Although Hamilton was still relatively inexperienced his High School is by common consent one of the finest monuments of the Scottish Greek Revival, its massive stepped profile culminating most effectively in the Doric temple portico of the assembly hall, which is approached by an impressive array of open staircases. That Hamilton had a mind as original as it was perceptive is shown by the handling of his two other principal Edinburgh commissions. As seen at the Dean Orphanage (1831–3) the attempt to combine neo-classical and baroque elements in direct apposition can hardly be judged a success, but at Physicians' Hall (1844–6) a similar fusion of styles, managed with greater finesse, achieves real distinction.

Glasgow, too, was expanding rapidly at this period, both westwards up the slopes of Blythswood Hill and on the south side of the river, where a pair of pavilioned terraces designed by Peter Nicholson was begun as early as

70 Royal High School,
Edinburgh

1802. New public buildings also continued to appear in considerable numbers, the leading figures here being William Stark and David Hamilton. Stark, who died prematurely in 1813, was widely regarded as Scotland's most promising architect, and it is unfortunate that of the few buildings that he is known to have designed only a handful now survive. His lunatic asylum at Bell's Park (1809), perhaps the first in Britain to employ a radiating plan, has long since disappeared, while the no less advanced Court House (1809) second only to Smirke's Covent Garden Theatre in its use of a Greek Doric portico, has been almost entirely remodelled. Hamilton, the son of a Glasgow mason, was an even more versatile designer than Stark. From the Adam-Wyatt style evidenced by Hutcheson's Hospital (1802–5) he passed rapidly to pure Greek, adding a vast Corinthian portico and spire to an earlier mansion to form the Royal Exchange (1827), which effectively terminates one of the principal vistas of the city centre. Hamilton's Western Club (1841), on the other hand, is an Italianate design of great originality incorporating some characteristically Mannerist detail.

Although Hamilton is known mainly for his work in Glasgow he also played an important part in the development of Aberdeen, for it was under his direction that the construction of King Street and Union Street was successfully completed (1800–5), thus making it possible for the city to expand towards open country. Thereafter the honours were shared by two local men of great ability, John Smith and Archibald Simpson, both of whom well knew how to exploit the qualities of the light-grey Rubislaw granite that was so readily available. Smith, who for long held the post of city architect, was responsible among other works for the very pretty little Town's Schools (1841) and for the graceful North Church (1830), both in the Greek manner, although his attachment to Perpendicular Gothic also earned him the nickname of 'Tudor Johnnie'. Simpson, the more resourceful designer of the two, worked mainly in Greek and to him are due many of the city's finest public buildings, including the Music Hall (1820), the Old Infirmary (1833–40) and the New Market, with its uncompromising façade and remarkable galleried interior (1840–2, demolished).

Simpson was also a prolific designer of classical country houses, two of his most monumental compositions being Crimonmogate (for Charles Bannerman, c. 1825) and Stracathro (for Alexander Cruikshank, 1827–30), whose external grandeur is complemented by sumptuous interior decoration in paint, scagliola and marble. A decade earlier Robert Smirke, who was then experimenting with a simple cubical formula, designed two distinctive houses of this kind in Scotland at Kinmount (for the Marquess of Queensberry, 1812) and Whittinghame (for James Balfour, 1818), while at

71 New Market, Aberdeen

Camperdown, near Dundee (for the 1st Earl of Camperdown, 1824–8), his pupil William Burn, then at the outset of his career, produced an Ionic variant of one of the most notable monuments of the English Greek Revival, William Wilkins' Grange Park.

In Scotland, even more than in England, it is hard to say where Gothic Survival ends and Gothic Revival begins. Post-Reformation churches continued to display medieval characteristics well into the eighteenth century, and both Sir William Bruce and James Smith were prepared to design in the Baronial style when occasion demanded. It seems clear, however, that the credit for the erection of the first major neo-Gothic house in Scotland belongs to an English architect, Roger Morris, whose designs for the 3rd Duke of Argyll's new mansion at Inveraray were prepared in 1744. Inveraray Castle is a great square block with circular angle-towers and a clearstoryed central hall which rises above the main roofline as a battlemented keep. Apart from the crenellated parapets the only external Gothic features are the pointed windows and hood-moulds (the conical roofs of the towers are later additions), while the interiors (p. 115), as in so many Georgian Gothic houses, are almost entirely classical. Morris also drew up a scheme for Gothicising another of the Duke's houses, Rosneath (demolished), while in about 1757 John Adam produced an ambitious design for a courtyard-plan castle at Douglas (demolished), with external detail very similar to that at Inveraray, where he had earlier succeeded his father as Master of Works.

The 'Adam castles' that sprang up all over Scotland in the later eighteenth century differed greatly in character from these first essays, however, and were the invention not of John Adam, but of his younger brothers Robert and James. The early examples, such as Mellerstain (for George Baillie of Jerviswood, 1770–8), tend to be rather lifeless and box-like, but Wedderburn (for Patrick Home of Wedderburn, 1770–8), with its boldly-massed angle-towers, strikes a more powerful and dramatic note which resounds with increasing emphasis through the later castles. These employ a common vocabulary of decoration and nearly all have symmetrical plans and classical interiors; in some cases main block and offices are integrated in elaborate courtyard-layouts. Much of the ornamental detail seems to derive from the Roman fortifications and medieval castles of Italy and the Adriatic, but some is clearly of native inspiration. Battlemented towers and turrets, corbelled parapets, crosslet-loops and crow-stepped gables are the most characteristic features; windows are invariably round- or square-headed, the pointed arch being conspicuously absent. Culzean (for the 10th Earl of Cassillis, 1777–90) begins to explore the full romantic possibilities of the style, its boldness of massing gaining additional effect from the superb cliff-top situation, while Pitfour (1784) and Seton (1789–91) are compact and well-integrated designs in which castellated features are reduced to a minimum. Finally, at Stobs (1792) Adam built a charming miniature version of Seton, employing square instead of round turrets and surmounting

Scottish crowsteps with Latin-Cross finials.

72 Seton House, East Lothian

    Most castellated houses designed by other architects of the period are indebted in some measure to the work of the Adam brothers. John Paterson was responsible for a number of successful designs of which Monzie (for Colonel Campbell of Monzie, 1795; remodelled by Lorimer, 1908–12) is probably the best surviving example. The Elliot brothers adopted the Adam manner at Loudon (for the Countess of Loudon, 1804–11), but their most outstanding work, Taymouth, completed for the 4th Earl of Breadalbane in 1806–10, is modelled upon Inveraray. The interiors are Gothic, however, their most notable features being the elegant fan-vaulted staircase, decorated by Francis Bernasconi in about 1810, and the extravaganza of painted plasterwork devised by Gillespie Graham and Frederick Crace some 30 years later.

    The symmetry of early Georgian Gothic buildings imposed certain obvious limitations upon design, but with the development of the

Picturesque movement in landscape and architecture at the end of the eighteenth century architects began to exploit the potentialities of the deliberately irregular composition. At the same time stylistic horizons were widening, the neo-Gothic vocabulary being enlarged by the introduction of Tudor, Jacobean and native Scottish idioms interspersed by more exotic themes derived from Asia and the Continent.

The earliest asymmetrical Gothic houses in Scotland were the work of English architects. Tullichewan, near Dumbarton, erected to a design of Robert Lugar in about 1808, has recently been demolished, but a comparable product by the same architect stands close by, at Balloch (for John Buchanan, 1809), its most remarkable feature being the concave plan of the principal façade. William Atkinson, a pupil of James Wyatt, is represented by two important houses of this class, Scone Palace (1803–12) and Rossie Priory (1810, demolished), both in the monastic vein, and Sir Robert Smirke by a single major example, Kinfauns (1820–4), although in

73 Dunninald, Angus

contrast to Balloch irregularity of composition is, in all these cases, conceived primarily in terms of the picturesque grouping of individually symmetrical components.

The most prolific, if not the most accomplished, exponent of the irregular Gothic house in Scotland was undoubtedly Gillespie Graham. Born in Dunblane in 1776 James Gillespie (he added Graham to his name following his marriage to a local heiress) is said to have started life as a joiner, but much of his architectural experience seems to have been gained in the western isles, where he superintended estate works, including the building of churches, schools and inns, for the 2nd Lord MacDonald during the first quarter of the nineteenth century. Graham's designs tended to be repetitive, but he was adept at devising rich Gothic interiors which are noticeably more authentic in character than those produced by the majority of his contemporaries. Duns (for William Hay, 1818–22) and Dunninald (for Peter Arkley, 1823–4) rank among the best examples of Graham's

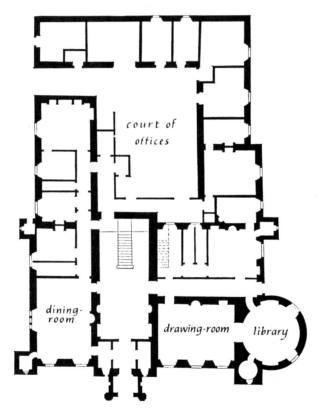

74 Dunninald, Angus: plan

castellated style, while his ecclesiastical Gothic is most eloquently represented at Cambusnethan (for Robert Lockhart of Castlehill, 1819), where crocketed finials and traceried windows are blended with fortified elements to produce a distinctly secular brand of monasticism. Graham was also a notable designer of Gothic churches, his most effective composition probably being Tolbooth St John's, Edinburgh, where he may have been assisted by his friend A. W. N. Pugin.

Richard Crichton, an Edinburgh architect who had trained under the Adam brothers and was a highly competent classicist, also designed a number of Georgian Gothic houses, the most outstanding of which was Abercairny (1804–42, demolished), a sumptuous essay in the abbey style. Following Crichton's premature death the interiors of Abercairny were completed by his nephews, Richard and Robert Dickson, who also produced several Gothic houses of their own, including the exquisitely detailed Millearne (1820–45, demolished). Millearne was executed in the Tudor style, which had been introduced into Scotland by William Wilkins at Dalmeny (1815–19) and taken up by William Burn (p. 158) at Blairquhan (1820-4) and Garscube (1826–7, demolished). Some of the most effective compositions in this style are to be found among houses of quite modest size, such as Smirke's uncompromisingly austere Cultoquhey (1818–22) and, at the opposite extreme, Robert Lugar's spirited Hensol (before 1828), with its sparkling granite masonry, ogee-roofed turrets and vistaed interiors.

Lugar was also responsible for an interesting Italianate house, Glenlee (1822), while a similar broad-eaved 'Campagna' style was employed to considerable effect by Archibald Simpson at Thainston (c. 1820–30), and by the Angus architect David Whyte, at Keithick (1818–23). Among the more interesting examples of contemporary work in other styles mention may be made of David Hamilton's 'Norman Castle' at Lennox (1837–41), and, representing the small rustic villa of Picturesque taste, the charming *cottage ornée* at Stuckgowan. Abbotsford (Edward Blore and William Atkinson, 1816–23), with its angle-turrets and crowsteps, foreshadows the early Victorian revival of the Scottish Baronial style, while the strapworked pediments and tall clustered chimneys of Dunlop (David Hamilton, 1833) proclaim a similar re-awakening of interest in the domestic architecture of the early Scottish Renaissance.

Some of the most important churches of the later Georgian period have already been noticed and space forbids mention of many more. One of the most attractive is St Andrew's, Dundee, erected by Samuel Bell, a local architect, in 1772 to plans prepared by James Craig of Edinburgh. The steeple, like many others of its kind, follows the pattern first introduced in the London city churches, while the classical detail is equally old fashioned. Several of the best oblong steepled churches are found in the smaller towns, those at Catrine (1792) and Fochabers (John Baxter, younger, 1797) having been planned to conform with 'new town' layouts. The galleried hall kirk, with or without a tower, remained extremely popular and although many of these buildings were of sadly pedestrian design there is no shortage of competent examples of both neo-classical and Gothic type, such as those produced over several decades by the Stirling family of Dunblane. Other plans were employed more sparingly, the octagon form appearing in classical dress at Kelso (James Nisbet, 1773) and in Gothic at St Paul's, Perth

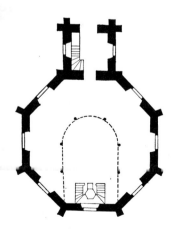

75 Glenorchy Church, Argyll: plan

(John Paterson, 1807) and Glenorchy (James Elliot, 1810), and the oval at St Andrew's, Edinburgh (Andrew Frazer, 1785), whose elegant steeple (William Sibbald, 1789) has become one of the most familiar landmarks of the New Town.

Laird's Houses

About the time of the Act of Union a new type of medium-sized domestic residence made its appearance in Scotland. Modelled, no doubt, mainly upon the classical mansions of Bruce and his followers the typical house of this class is a plain oblong gable-roofed block of two main storeys and an attic having a symmetrical plan in which a single large room is placed on either side of a central staircase on each floor. More accommodation is sometimes obtained by the addition of a basement, or by increasing the width of the building so that two rooms can be placed on each side of the stair. The symmetry of the plan is clearly reflected in the elevations, particularly in the main front, where the windows are invariably regularly disposed about a central entrance.

The small symmetrically-designed house quickly found favour in all parts of the country, becoming the standard form of residence not only of the lowland laird and highland tacksman, but also of the parish minister, of the merchant and master-craftsman in the provincial burgh and, ultimately, of the prosperous farmer. An early and well-preserved example of the simplest kind of laird's dwelling can be seen at Auchentroig, Stirlingshire, a county which contains several similar houses of early- and mid-eighteenth-century date. Erected for John MacLachlan in 1702 Auchentroig measures only 37ft. by 19ft. over all, one of the two ground-floor rooms forming a parlour and the other a kitchen with a large arched fireplace. In general, houses varied little in appearance from one part of the country to another. Old Holylee (1734), the residence of a Border laird, bears a strong family resemblance to its contemporaries in central Scotland, and the same is true of the majority of comparable buildings in the highlands. In most cases the builders of houses such as these must have been only too glad to pull down their previous dwellings, since these were frequently primitive or antiquated. The laird of Hills, however, already the possessor of a fine late medieval tower-house, preferred to make the best of both worlds and by placing his compactly-planned house of 1721 hard against one wall of the old tower cast himself in the dual role of castellan and country gentleman; a similar juxtaposition occurs at Bonshaw and Auchanachy.

These houses could provide only a very limited amount of accommodation, most of them containing no more than four main apartments. More space could readily be found, however, by elongating the main block, an arrangement that enabled the principal rooms to be either enlarged in size or increased in number. Hilton (1732) provides a good example of this development, additional smaller rooms being contrived on each side of the staircase, which for once loses its central position. A somewhat similar

76 Old Auchentroig, Stirlingshire

77 Hills Tower,
Kirkcudbrightshire

arrangement occurs at Greenhill (now being reconstructed to form part of
Biggar Museum), while at Braes, Stirlingshire, a mid-eighteenth-century
reconstruction of an earlier house enabled three main rooms to be provided
on each of the two principal floors with a fourth behind the stair. Most of
these houses have three- or five-window fronts, but Dunbarney has six
windows and the exceptionally long Brightmony (c. 1732) eight windows
An alternative method of obtaining more accommodation was by the
adoption of a T-plan, the additional limb being utilised to house either the
staircase or an extra room. Two Aberdeenshire houses, Faichfield (c. 1700,
demolished) and Nether Ardgrain (1731), illustrate this arrangement, the

former also incorporating a third full storey. Occasionally, as at Skellater, a fine early-eighteenth-century house of the Forbes family, two wings were added to the main block to form a half-H plan reminiscent of those found in the preceding century (p. 57).

Larger versions of the standard type of laird's house, in which the main block was increased in width so as to accommodate two rooms on each side of the staircase, began to appear about the second quarter of the eighteenth century. One of the earliest and best preserved is Glen (1734), where the conventional five-window front is dignified by rusticated quoins and a moulded eaves-course. Occasionally a satisfactory plan of this type could be contrived within the framework of an older building. Dunbarney, for instance, was doubled in width towards the end of the eighteenth century by the erection of a second range of apartments behind the long narrow block of the original house.

In many cases these houses of double-room width were equipped with service basements, their standards of accommodation being equivalent to those of a small mansion. Forebank and Gourdie provide excellent illustrations of this type of arrangement. Each is a gable-roofed block comprising a basement, two main storeys and an attic, and each has a symmetrical internal layout about an internal stair. At Forebank (1757), where the stair is at the rear, the 'double-pile' nature of the plan is emphasized by the central corridor that traverses the long axis of the house at first-floor level, giving access to rooms in each corner of the building. The great majority of these houses were gable-roofed and gable-chimneyed, hipped-roof houses having chimneys in the two mid-partitions being a good deal less common, although this was a standard arrangement in larger country mansions. Two Ayrshire houses, Greenan and Drumburle, illustrate this form, however, while Dalquhairn, Stirlingshire, is gable-ended but with chimneys in the mid-walls. Lochlane (1710) is a fine hip-roofed building of T-plan having a four-window front with attic dormers. As in many other houses of this class there seem originally to have been single-storeyed wings extending forward from the corners of the main block to form a courtyard.

The provision of a suitable residence for the minister was a responsibility of the heritors and the standard of accommodation supplied varied a good deal from one parish to another. Literary evidence shows that many seventeenth- and early-eighteenth-century manses, particularly in the highlands, were very mean, although the more fortunate ministers of the eastern lowlands were sometimes housed in buildings similar in character to those occupied by the smaller heritors. After the Union, however, the majority of new manses were modelled upon one or other of the smaller versions of the symmetrically-planned laird's house, and buildings of this type continued to be erected well into the Victorian era. Standardisation is especially well marked in the highlands, where a very large number of new churches and manses were erected in late Georgian times. Donald Sage,

78 Forebank,
Kincardineshire

minister of Resolis, relates that all the manses constructed in Sutherland and Ross between 1760 and 1804 were of uniform design (the plans being supplied by James Boag of Dornoch) with 'the usual number of chimneys, namely two, rising like asses' ears at either end, and ensuring the purpose for which they were designed as ill as usual'. Better known, perhaps, are Thomas Telford's 'parliamentary manses', of which about 40 were constructed in the highlands during the second quarter of the nineteenth century to standard plans, one for a two-storeyed T-plan building and the other for a more modest single-storeyed building of H-plan.

Dovecots

In a land where food was often difficult to obtain and winter menus could show little variety pigeons made a welcome addition to the table and most people of any consequence had their own dovecot. The flocks fed indiscriminately, preying not only upon the crops of the proprietor, but also upon those of unprivileged tenants, and it is not surprising that severe penalties were laid down for those found destroying dovecots or shooting pigeons.

Most Scottish dovecots are small plain buildings of stone, their walls being pierced only by an entrance and a few ventilation-slits. In most cases one or more continuous string-courses are set out a few feet above ground-level – a device probably intended to prevent rats and other vermin from gaining access. Entry-holes for the pigeons are usually contrived within the roof, while the whole of the interior is lined with nesting-boxes, reached by means of a 'potence', or revolving ladder. The oldest surviving dovecots, which belong to the sixteenth century, are of 'bee-hive' type, being circular in plan with gently tapering walls and flat domed roofs. These were succeeded during the following century by the 'lectern' type, so called because of its rectangular plan and distinctive lean-to roof; the pigeon-ports are nearly always placed midway down the roof, while the characteristic crowsteps make excellent perches. Before the agrarian improvements of the late Georgian period rendered it obsolete, however, the Scottish dovecot passed through yet a third phase of development characterised by the introduction of new materials, particularly local brick.

Industrial Buildings

Scotland's possession of extensive mineral resources and an abundance of sites suitable for harnessing water power ensured her an important role in the Industrial Revolution, while at the same time her topography presented tremendous challenges in the field of communications. In the development of the country's two chief industries of textile manufacture and metallurgy much of the initiative came from England, through the agency of men like Arkwright and Garbett, but for the task of road and bridge building and for the construction of canals, harbours and lighthouses, Scotland produced engineers whose inventive genius restored the balance in full measure.

79 Perth Waterworks

The pace of technological change varied widely from one branch of manufacture to another. Thus, the old established linen trade remained primarily a cottage industry until well into the nineteenth century, spinning and weaving usually being done by hand as a part-time occupation. The cotton industry, on the other hand, developed with exceptional rapidity, new and improved types of spinning machinery becoming available just at the time when Scotland's trade was being re-orientated following the economic disasters brought about by the American War of Independence. Within a decade of the establishment of the first effective cotton-mills at Penicuik and Rothesay in 1778 some 20 mills were in operation, and there were more than twice this number before the end of the century. The most famous of these early enterprises were the New Lanark Mills, founded by Richard Arkwright and David Dale in 1785 and managed by the latter's son-in-law, Robert Owen, from 1799 to 1827. The village of New Lanark is one of the outstanding monuments of the Industrial Revolution in Britain, the close interrelationship of its mills, schools, shops and workers' model dwellings reflecting the founders' ideal of a planned community governed by the principles of philanthropic socialism. Second only in interest are the Stanley Cotton Mills, established in the same year as New Lanark by a group of local gentry and merchants, together with Arkwright, upon land feued from another supporter, the Duke of Atholl. The existing buildings include a six-storeyed mill of stone and brick construction which, like its companions, was powered by giant water-wheels supplied through a tunnel that drew the waters of the Tay from beyond Shiel Hill. The floors of these

80 New Lanark, Lanarkshire

early mills were invariably of timber construction, making them disastrously vulnerable to fire, but from the early nineteenth century onwards it became customary to incorporate an internal framework of fireproof construction. Houldsworth's Cotton Mill, Glasgow (1804–5, demolished) was the first industrial building in Scotland to be constructed in this way, the floors being carried upon brick arches and cast-iron beams and columns, which also served as heating-pipes.

Iron smelting by means of primitive 'bloomery' furnaces was carried out in many parts of Scotland from an early date, but the recent history of the industry begins with the foundation of the Glen Kinglass furnace in 1725. Like its successors at Invergarry (1727), Bonawe (1753) and Goatfield (1755) this enterprise was an offshoot of the Lancashire iron industry, the ore being transported by sea from these areas to the highlands, whose abundant woodlands could provide the furnace charcoal that was by this time difficult to obtain elsewhere. The most notable surviving remains are at Bonawe, where there may be seen an early industrial layout as self-contained as that of New Lanark, the furnace itself standing in close proximity to iron-ore and charcoal storage-sheds, while nearby there are rows of flatted dwellings, a manager's house and a pier and storehouse. The general adoption of coke fuel in place of charcoal during the second half of the eighteenth century led to the large-scale establishment of the industry in the central lowlands, where both ironstone and coal were readily available. Carron Ironworks was founded by Samuel Garbett and two Scottish co-partners in 1759, to be followed after an interval of 20 years by a coke-furnace at Wilsontown and thereafter by other works in different places. At Carron itself all the original buildings have been replaced, but an important early nineteenth-century engineering-shop survives, while Wilsontown, Muirkirk and Shotts all retain interesting early remains.

Other industries, too, have left their legacy of early buildings. Mining and quarrying, for example, have led to the existence of villages in places as remote as Leadhills and Wanlockhead, as well as to the scatter of abandoned limekilns that today confronts the visitor to the Lothians. At Whitehills, on the Banffshire coast, traditional methods of fireclay manufacture were until recently employed by the Blackpots Brick and Tile Works, the clay being processed by a hand-operated machine and dried by natural ventilation before being fired in a kiln. By the 1830s gas lighting was being installed in many Scottish burghs and early gasworks survive in some of the smaller towns, such as Biggar and Lauder, while Perth still retains the exceptionally fine waterworks (1830–2) designed by Adam Anderson, complete with domed cast-iron storage tank and columnar stone chimney.

Scotland's first canal is supposed to have been constructed in the reign of James IV by that doughty sea captain Sir Andrew Wood of Largo so that he could sail to church each Sunday in his barge. The aims of those who subsequently established the main Scottish canal network were rather more prosaic, many of the earliest waterways, such as the Monkland Canal

(1770–3) being intended primarily for the transport of coal. The Forth and Clyde Canal, begun under the direction of John Smeaton in 1768, was designed to facilitate commerce between the eastern and western lowlands at a time of rapid industrial expansion. The terrain was unusually difficult, necessitating massive embankments in some sections, while conditions were little more favourable for the later construction of an eastwards extension to Edinburgh, known as the Union Canal (Hugh Baird, 1818–22), which included a rock-cut tunnel and several major aqueducts. Formidable as these problems were, however, they were nothing to those that confronted Thomas Telford during the construction of the Caledonian Canal (1814–22). At the south end of the canal the steep ascent to Loch Lochy involved the building of no less than eight gigantic locks (promptly christened 'Neptune's Staircase'), while at the north end the entrance to the large Clachnaharry Basin had to be founded upon piles more than 60ft. deep.

81 Blackpots Brick and Tile Works, Banffshire

82 Avon Aqueduct, Union Canal, Stirlingshire

Apart from a few primitive beacon-towers, like that on May Island (1636), in the Firth of Forth, no lighthouses were built round the Scottish coast prior to the establishment of the Board of Commissioners of Northern Lighthouses in 1786. The earliest of the Commissioners' lighthouses, erected in the following year, was no more than a tower perched on the roof of a sixteenth-century castle standing upon Kinnaird Head, but more ambitious projects soon followed, the most notable being the construction of the Bell Rock Lighthouse off Arbroath in 1807–11. Credit for the design, which was modelled upon that of the Eddystone Lighthouse, belongs primarily to Robert Stevenson, the Commissioners' engineer, who benefited from the advice of John Rennie. Great difficulties were encountered, the Inchcape reef being exposed for such short periods that no more than a few hours' work was possible each day, and that only during the summer months; the tower rises to a height of 127ft., the greater part of the masonry being of dovetail-joint construction. Among the most impressive of the other Scottish lighthouses of the period are Rhinns of Islay (1823–5), also designed by Stevenson, and Skerryvore (1840–4), one of the principal achievements of the engineer's eldest son, Alan Stevenson.

The earliest surviving Scottish bridges, which date from the fifteenth and early sixteenth centuries, are characterised by narrow roadways, massive piers and multiple arches of limited span. The bridges at Dumfries, Ayr and Stirling belong to this period, and likewise those at Haddington and Bridge of Dee, Aberdeen, which employ ribbed arches, as well as one or two single-arched structures such as Brig-o'Doon, Ayr. Few major bridges were erected during the century following the Reformation, but with the growth of coach traffic towards the end of the seventeenth century building was commenced on a more extensive scale, the number of bridges multiplying during the following century as the military road-system was driven into the Highlands and the Turnpike Acts introduced. At the same time carriageways became wider and arch spans were increased, while piers and cut-waters gradually assumed more slender proportions.

One of the best of the improved bridges is Clydesholm Bridge (1694–9), a plain three-arched structure designed by John Lockart of Lanark, while Hyndford Bridge and Bridge of Dun (Alexander Stevens, 1773 and 1785–7), with their roadways and developed cutwaters, exemplify the more sophisticated approach of the bridge builders of the turnpike era. Most of the numerous military bridges are severely plain, but the most famous of them, General Wade's Bridge at Aberfeldy (William Adam, 1733), is an elaborate structure of some architectural distinction. The erection of Smeaton's handsome nine-arch bridge at Perth (1766–72) marked the opening of a new era of bridge building dominated by the great engineers of the late Georgian period. Smeaton himself followed up his achievement at Perth with similarly designed bridges at Coldstream (1766) and Lower North Water (1775) while Rennie built the extremely influential Kelso Bridge (1803), whose elegant semi-elliptical arches, twin-columned piers and level roadway were soon echoed at Waterloo Bridge, London, and elsewhere. But the greatest individual contribution was undoubtedly that of Telford, who was personally responsible for the design and execution of many of the bridges erected by the Commission of Highland Roads and Bridges after 1803, including the fine seven-arch bridge across the Tay at Dunkeld (1809) which opened up the whole of the central highlands, and the beautiful cast-iron Spey Bridge (1815) at Craigellachie. Credit for the construction of the first large British suspension-bridge must go not to Telford, however, but to Sir Samuel Brown, who having taken out a patent for bridges of this type in 1817, spanned the Tweed at Hutton in 1820, the year before work began on Telford's Menai Suspension Bridge. This pioneer structure, which still carries traffic across the Border, has a length of 361ft. and the total weight of 100 tons is carried on three main double chains of flat-link construction.

83 Hutton Suspension
Bridge, Berwickshire

5
Victorian Transformation

In Scotland, as in many other parts of Britain, the Victorian age was predominantly a period of rapid and widespread change. Political, social and intellectual life was profoundly modified at every level. While new links were forged overseas through trade and colonization old bonds were severed at home, not least in ecclesiastical affairs, where church reform was achieved only at the cost of schism. During the course of the nineteenth century the population multiplied almost threefold, while at the same time there was a marked movement away from rural areas, particularly the highlands, towards the developing urban centres of the central lowlands. Here the long established cotton trade continued to flourish, at least in the west, until about the 1880s, by which time the lead had passed to the new jute and woollen manufactures of the east coast and the Borders. The most outstanding feature of Scotland's economic development, however, was the rise of the heavy industries of the Clyde Valley, where the ready availability of coal and iron fostered shipbuilding and engineering enterprises which themselves both contributed to and benefited from the simultaneous expansion of the canal system and the advent of the railway.

Many of these developments led directly to some form of building activity. The newfound wealth of industrialists and leaders of commerce was employed in the erection of country houses and lavish suburban dwellings, while before the onset of depression in the late 1870s agricultural prosperity likewise encouraged the traditional land-owning classes to rebuild their family seats and to provide handsome new farmhouses and steadings for their tenants. The Disruption of 1843, many of whose supporters were as rich as they were zealous, inaugurated a period of church building on a scale unparalleled since the high Middle Ages. Improvements in communications could scarcely be achieved without the construction of large numbers of bridges, harbours, railway stations and hotels, while each expanding industry required its own complement of factories and warehouses and often, as in the case of the collieries, workers' houses as well. But it was, of course, in the towns and cities of the industrial belt, where the pace of change was swiftest, that the greatest transformation took place.

The Towns

By the beginning of the nineteenth century Glasgow had established itself as one of the leading commercial and manufacturing centres of Britain and during the next few decades the city's growth was phenomenal, the population quadrupling itself before 1850 and rising to more than three quarters of a million by the end of the century. Quite early in the Victorian period the first and second Georgian new towns, lying immediately to the west of the medieval centre, started to become commercialized as their more prosperous residents moved further out towards the leafy slopes of Woodside and Kelvingrove, while south of the river, too, new suburbs began to spring up round Queen's Park, leaving the less well off to find accommodation in the tenements of Lauriston and the Gorbals.

Apart from J. T. Rochead, whose boldly Italianate Grosvenor Terrace (1855) made a notable individual contribution, the principal architects of this phase of the city's growth were Charles Wilson and Alexander Thomson. Wilson, the son of a local builder, had worked in David Hamilton's office for ten years before setting up in business on his own account in 1837. Thereafter he built up a large and varied practice throughout the west of Scotland and beyond, much of his best work being executed in Glasgow itself, where he became President of the Institute of Architects. In his own day Wilson won recognition as much for his country houses and churches as for his street architecture, but today it is for the latter, in particular the superbly conceived Woodlands Hill scheme (1855–7), carried out in association with Sir Joseph Paxton's development of the adjacent Kelvingrove Park, that the architect is chiefly remembered. The contrast between the solid Georgian dignity of the hill-top Park Circus and the thrusting Victorian assertion of the encircling Park Terrace is singularly effective, the whole composition being crowned by the triple towers of the picturesque Free Church College (1856). In the composition of this latter building Wilson combined architectural themes of widely differing origin in a highly original way, a tactic that he repeated to even greater effect in the remarkable Queen's Rooms (1857, now a Christian Science Church) which takes the form of classical temple in Germanic Cinquecento dress.

Thompson, who in due course followed Wilson as President of the Glasgow Institute of Architects, was active mainly in the southern suburbs of the city, where his work bears the strong personal stamp that characterizes his architectural output as a whole. Meticulously composed and exquisitely detailed, these mid-century terraces can now be recognized as among the most advanced undertakings of their kind. But although their celebrated 'Greekness' proves on close examination to be superficial, they certainly do not lack a classical severity which in some cases makes them rather uninviting as residences. Thomson also built a number of ingeniously conceived villas in and around Glasgow, but his best-known works are undoubtedly the city churches in Caledonia Road (1856) and St Vincent

84 Queen's Rooms,
Glasgow.

85 St Vincent Street
Church, Glasgow

Street (1858), which are monumental compositions of great power and originality; a third church of even more idiosyncratic design (Queen's Park, 1867) was destroyed during the Second World War.

The decorous terraces of Woodside and Strathbungo are by no means typical of nineteenth-century housing in Glasgow, however, for the majority of tradesmen and artisans – and not a few middle-class families as well – lived in the three-, four- or five-storeyed tenements that still predominate in many parts of the city. The best of these are dignified and unpretentious, the embodiment of the Victorian ideals of thrift and self-help, but even the most skilful architects found it difficult to avoid monotony and many of the products of local builders were distinctly dreary.

The period that saw the growth of the western and southern suburbs also brought great changes to the city centre, where the demands of commerce and administration soon led to further building, some of it on a fairly lavish scale. Among these new edifices warehouses and banks were especially prominent, the former being well represented by Gardner's, Jamaica Street (1855–6), an iron-framed structure designed by John Baird, a local architect of strong practical talent who had roofed the nearby Argyle Arcade with an exposed iron frame of hammerbeam type as early as 1827. Alexander Thomson, who had worked in Baird's office, was also responsible for a number of important warehouses, including the Buck's Head, Argyle Street (1863), which combines cast iron and glass with equal elegance and candour, and the remarkable Egyptian Halls, Union Street (1871–3), where, in contrast, the glazing is integrated within a masonry framework, the top storey comprising an almost continuous glass screen set behind a free-standing colonnade.

For banks the Renaissance palazzo was generally considered to provide the most suitable model, one or two of the most opulent examples (Commercial Bank, Gordon Street, 1857) being the work of the Edinburgh architect David Rhind. Charles Wilson also produced several well conceived commercial and institutional buildings in the Italianate manner (Royal Faculty of Procurators, St George's Place, 1854), and the fashion was continued by architects of the next generation such as John Burnet, senior. All the leading designers of this period were accustomed to work in a variety of styles, however, and Burnet was also responsible for one of the most scholarly of Glasgow's Greek churches (Elgin Place Congregational, 1856), while his younger contemporary James Sellars, working very much in the manner of Thomson, produced at Kelvinside Academy (1877) a neo-classical composition of quite unexpected severity.

The Gothic Revival style, in contrast, never found much favour in Glasgow, a circumstance which can hardly be attributed to provincialism since both Edinburgh and Aberdeen adopted the new fashion with alacrity. Its unpopularity is the more surprising in view of the fact that no less an exponent of the Gothic vocabulary than Thomas Rickman was commis-

86 Gardner's
Warehouse, Glasgow

sioned to design an English Decorated church in Ingram Street in 1824, while Gillespie Graham's pioneering Catholic Chapel (now the Roman Catholic cathedral) was begun as early as 1814. Both these churches were much admired in their day, but they had few successors until after 1850, the best of these probably being the Barony Church, Castle Street (Sir John Burnet and J. A. Campbell, 1886), a fine Early Pointed composition with a most impressive interior on the Gerona model. John Honeyman and William Leiper, both of whom had trained in England, likewise designed several excellent Gothic churches, the former also making his mark elsewhere in Scotland as a restorer.

So far as secular buildings are concerned, the principal monument of the

87 Glasgow University

88 Athenaeum Theatre,
Glasgow

Gothic Revival is the University, which was transplanted to Gilmorehill in 1870, its handsome seventeenth-century predecessor in the old city being sacrificed to make way for a railway goods-yard. Sir George Gilbert Scott's design evidently stems from the late medieval cloth halls of Flanders and does not look altogether at home in Kelvingrove, although the openwork spire (1887), redesigned for the central tower by his son, certainly makes the building one of Glasgow's most prominent landmarks.

Although each successive phase of the city's development had brought to light local architects of great ability, the late Victorian and Edwardian eras discovered a galaxy of talent which made Glasgow for a short time one of the foremost architectural centres of Europe. The leading names were those of the younger Burnet, Campbell, the younger Salmon and Mackintosh. Sir John Burnet's early work reflects his Paris Beaux Arts training, but following a visit to the United States in 1896 he began to experiment with a more functional style in which the underlying steel framework of a building was increasingly allowed to govern the composition of the façade, a development which was in due course to lead to his extremely influential design for the Kodak building in London. Burnet also succeeded in finding a satisfactory formula for the tall narrow-fronted buildings that commercial pressures (and the introduction of the elevator) were imposing upon the city centre, working in close association with J. A. Campbell, who was a partner in the firm from 1886 to 1897. One of the earliest of these strongly vertical compositions was the former Athenaeum Theatre, Buchanan Street (1891), whose unorthodox but well-integrated window treatment provided a basis for much of Campbell's later work.

James Salmon, born like Burnet into one of Glasgow's leading architectural families, produced his own version of the soaring bay-window theme. His well known 'Hatrack' (142 St Vincent Street, 1899), which rises to a height of ten storeys on a frontage of less than 30 feet, is a masterpiece of ingenuity, while at Lion Chambers, Hope Street (1906), he adopted an advanced form of reinforced concrete construction (devised by L. G. Mouchel of the Hennebique Co.) which made possible the introduction of membrane walls and floors only four inches in thickness.

But the supreme formulation of vertical design did not make its appearance until the following year, when work began on the library wing of Charles Rennie Mackintosh's Glasgow School of Art. Mackintosh's competition design for the School had been accepted in 1896, but financial difficulties made it necessary to carry out the work in stages, the Renfrew Street front, with its considered asymmetry and idiosyncratic detail, being completed only in 1907 and the library itself two years later. Mackintosh is now recognized as a designer of rare if at times unfathomable genius, and although his School of Art is perhaps not the most famous of Glasgow's buildings it is deservedly the most highly regarded.

Although Glasgow and Edinburgh lie little more than 40 miles apart the Victorian architecture of the two cities differs markedly in character, and

89 Glasgow School of
Art

few even of the leading architects of the period practised widely in both
cities. Edinburgh, as already noted, embraced the Gothic Revival more
wholeheartedly than Glasgow, whose later commercial architecture has no
real counterpart in the capital and where neo-Greek, surprisingly, lingered a
good deal longer.

Edinburgh's New Town, like Glasgow's, continued to expand rapidly
during the early Victorian period and before the coming of the railway
called a halt, the Calton Hill and West End schemes were well advanced and

a start had been made on the development of the Learmonth Estate, which had been linked to the West End by the construction of Telford's bridge across the Water of Leith in 1832. As a study of the West End scheme shows, Georgian concepts of design were slow to be abandoned. The simple grid and crescent layout of the earlier phases of the New Town was followed throughout, while the differences between Robert Brown's Melville Street (1820–6) and later streets by John Chesser and others are largely those of emphasis and detail. Nor was the essential unity of the scheme threatened even when the stately mass of Sir George Gilbert Scott's Episcopal cathedral of St Mary began to rise on a focal site at the west end of Melville Street in 1874, and St Mary's triple Gothic spires (completed in 1917) now form the most memorable landmark of the city's western approaches.

Beyond the confines of the successive New Towns stood rows of middle-class and artisan tenements, geographically segregated but otherwise scarcely distinguishable, while further out high garden walls gave privacy to the comfortable suburban villas of Murrayfield and the Grange. The slums of the city centre, on the other hand, many of them buildings of high architectural quality which had once accommodated men of rank and fortune, were generally recognized as being among the worst in Europe. Even here, however, the various City Improvement Acts slowly brought about some amelioration, while elsewhere charitable societies and individuals promoted a number of model housing schemes, including Well Court (1884) in the Dean Village, founded by a local philanthropist, J. R. Findlay, and sensitively laid out by his architect Sydney Mitchell.

So far as public buildings were concerned Edinburgh was no less successful than Glasgow in recruiting local architects of talent, some of whom likewise became figures of national reputation. Prominent among the first generation of Victorian designers was David Bryce, son of an Edinburgh builder and pupil of William Burn, whose partner he became in 1841 (p. 160). Bryce was an energetic and resourceful designer of eclectic taste who composed fluently in a wide variety of styles. For many of his earlier commercial and institutional buildings, such as the Western Bank, St Andrew's Square (1846, demolished), he adopted the palazzo model, first introduced to the capital by Burn at the New Club (1834, demolished), but Bryce was also experimenting with neo-baroque as early as 1835 (St Mary's Unitarian Church, Castle Terrace), although his most effective composition in this vein, the richly modelled Bank of Scotland, on the Mound, was not begun until 1864. At Fettes College (1862), on the other hand, Bryce amplified one of the themes he had been developing in his country house practice (p. 161) to produce a full-blooded French Gothic design of great originality.

Less prolific in output but equally adept in his mastery of contemporary idiom was David Rhind, whose Life Association building in Princes Street (1855–8, demolished) marked the culmination of the palazzo style in Edinburgh and whose Graeco-Roman Commercial Bank (George Street,

90 Life Association
Building, Edinburgh

1846–7) rivals Bryce's neighbouring and contemporary Britsh Linen Bank (now Bank of Scotland), St Andrew's Square, in opulence. Robert Matheson, architect to the Office of Works, favoured a more restrained Italian style, elegantly displayed in his New Register House (1856–62) and General Post Office (1861–5). He also erected the monumental but somewhat overscale Royal Scottish Museum (1861–74), whose Renaissance façade encloses a remarkable galleried hall of cast iron and glass devised by Francis Fowke RE (of South Kensington fame), the principal architect of the building.

In the background there were a host of lesser figures, some like G. M. Kemp, the ill-fated designer of the Scott Monument in Princes Street (1840–6), recognized for a single major achievement, others like Sir James Gowans and the English architect F. T. Pilkington celebrated chiefly for their originality. It is hard to decide whether Gowans, with his obsession with rational planning and modular construction (the masonry of his house in Edinburgh was constructed in accordance with a standard two-foot grid), should be regarded as a pioneer or an eccentric. But Pilkington's work, although uneven in quality, reveals an acute mind and extraordinary powers of expression, and his superbly composed Barclay Church (1862–4) ranks as one of the outstanding monuments of the Scottish Gothic Revival.

The dominant architectural practice in late Victorian Edinburgh, however, was that of Sir R. Rowand Anderson, whose initial experience had been gained in the Royal Engineers, where he had had the opportunity to assist in R. W. Billings's restoration work at Edinburgh Castle. He also came under the influence of Sir George Gilbert Scott, who in 1862 commissioned him to superintend the erection of St James's Episcopal Church, Leith. It was an opportune time for Anderson to begin his professional career, for the death of John Henderson in that year had robbed Scotland of one of its foremost church architects, whose designs for Trinity College, Glenalmond (1841–51), St Mary's, Arbroath (1854) and numerous other Episcopalian churches had opened the country to the full influence of the English Tractarian Gothic school. At first Anderson's practice was devoted mainly to church building, but following a brief partnership with David Bryce in 1873 he broadened his range and soon began to attract many commissions from private individuals and institutions. Although conceived in a variety of styles his work was invariably scholarly and well composed and in Edinburgh itself Anderson was responsible for a number of distinguished public buildings including the richly detailed Gothic Scottish National Portrait Gallery (1885–90) and the University's McEwan Hall (1887–97), an impressive and well-sited piece of architecture in the High Renaissance manner. In the design of this latter project Anderson was assisted by G. Washington Browne, another accomplished and erudite designer who showed himself well able to work in the more expansive idiom of his own day. Browne's particular fondness for the François Ier style is well demonstrated by his very lively Public Library

91 Trinity College,
Glenalmond

(George IV Bridge, 1887–90), with its lavish sculpturework and jaunty
lantern.

Unlike Glasgow and Edinburgh, Dundee did not produce many local
architects of distinction, and at least until the closing decades of the
Victorian era most of the major commissions went to outsiders. During the
rapid expansion of the city in the 1820s and 1830s one of the leading figures
was the Edinburgh architect George Angus, who laid out Reform Street,
using the Greek Doric portico of his own High School (1832–4) as a terminal
feature. It was Angus, too, who won the competition design for a new gaol
and courthouse (1833, courthouse completed 1863), while the other major
neo-classical public building of the period, the imposing Custom House
(1842–3) was the joint-product of the local Harbour Engineer, John Leslie,
and John Taylor, of Glasgow.

By this time Dundee was feeling the effects of industrial depression, but
the opening of the second half of the century brought a return to prosperity
and building soon recommenced on a still wider scale. In 1852 a new and
extensive Infirmary was begun to an able design in the Tudor manner by
Messrs Coe and Godwin while in 1867 another London architect, Sir G. G.

Scott, who had already built St Paul's Episcopal Church (1853–5, now the Cathedral), produced the boldly conceived but poorly detailed Albert Institute. Two other notable Gothic Revival buildings of this period were Bryce's handsome Royal Exchange (1853–6) and Peddie and Kinnear's Morgan Hospital (1863–6), while among the churches mention should be made of G. F. Bodley's St Salvador's Episcopal (1865–74), which combines simplicity of form with rich interior decoration in gesso, stencilwork and painted glass.

Except in the sphere of domestic architecture, the late Victorian period, although prodigal in output, produced little to compare in quality or interest with what had gone before. Not, of course, that jute palaces and suburban villas were new phenomena in Dundee, for a number of sizeable mansions had been constructed in the western outskirts of the city by Charles Wilson of Glasgow in the 1850s, while shortly afterwards Andrew Heiton's vast and showy Castleroy (1867, demolished) set the tone for Broughty Ferry. Even Castleroy, however, could scarcely match the Franco-

92 St Salvador's Episcopal Church, Dundee. Interior

Scottish splendours of Carbet Castle (T. S. Robertson, c. 1870), erected in the same neighbourhood a little later for a rival family, but destined, like many of its kind, to survive little longer than the generation who built it. During the same period a drastic programme of slum clearance initiated by the Burgh Engineer, William Mackison, made a fairly clean sweep of the historic buildings of the city centre, which was soon laid out with undistinguished streets of shops and offices.

Aberdeen, geographically remote from the cities of the lowland belt and further isolated by the distinctive properties of her building stone, found no difficulty in retaining her architectural identity. It comes as no surprise to find that during the Victorian period building activity in the 'Granite City' was dominated by two or three family dynasties of local architects, and by a no less closely knit circle of quarry masters and craftsmen who alone possessed the skill to translate concept into reality. At the beginning of the period Smith and Simpson (p. 118) were still very much in command, and the latter's East and Belmont Church, originally a group of three separate Disruption churches united beneath a remarkable brick spire of German form, was not completed until shortly before his death in 1847. Smith's son William, who took over his father's practice, also produced a number of Gothic buildings, including a replacement spire for St Nicholas's Church (1878–80) and a block in Union Street (1846) which is said to have made a highly favourable impression upon Prince Albert, thus leading to Smith's being commissioned to design Balmoral Castle. Later in the century one of Smith's pupils, William Kelly, brought a fuller understanding to the interpretation of the medieval styles, both in his new work, as in the restrained Scots Gothic St Ninian's Church (1898) and in his restorations, notably at the crypt of St Nicholas's (1898) and at King's College Chapel (1931). Kelly's classical work was equally scholarly, however, as demonstrated by his Aberdeen Savings banks in Union Terrace (1896) and George Street (1905), which are composed and executed with great fastidiousness.

The other major figure of the late Victorian period was A. Marshall Mackenzie, son of the able Thomas Mackenzie of Elgin (who had trained under Archibald Simpson) and nephew of William M. Mackenzie, city architect of Perth. Mackenzie, who at first practised in association with his father's former partner, James Matthews (himself the possessor of one of the largest practices in the country), had an extensive and varied output both in Aberdeen and beyond, becoming particularly well known for ecclesiastical work, most of which was in the Gothic idiom (e.g. Craigiebuckler Church, 1883). He also designed many notable commercial and institutional buildings, including the vigorous Renaissance Northern Assurance Building, Union Street (1885), which like most of the principal public buildings of the day was constructed of the silvery Kemnay granite from middle Donside, recently made available in bulk through the development of revolutionary quarrying techniques. The most famous of

Mackenzie's buildings in Aberdeen, however, is the Broad Street front of Marischal College (1903–6), a surprisingly successful English Perpendicular composition which also constitutes a high watermark in granite craftsmanship.

Industry and Communications

Although the textile industry did not occupy as dominant a position in Scotland's economy during the Victorian era as in previous generations, some branches of manufacture continued to prosper. The introduction of jute gave a new lease of life to the linen trade and led to its rapid expansion in the Dundee area, where more than 60 mills were in operation by the 1860s. By this time the methods of fireproof construction that had been pioneered at the turn of the century in Glasgow (p. 132) and in Dundee itself (Bell Mill, 1806, demolished) were in general use, but the buildings themselves were often much larger, although few could match the Camperdown Works (1861–8), which extends to a length of 500 feet and incorporates a 280 foot chimney-stack designed by James MacLaren in the form of an Italian campanile. Other important centres of the linen trade that retain good examples of Victorian mills are Blairgowrie, Brechin and Arbroath, while Kirkcaldy specialized both in jute and flax spinning and, from about 1850 onwards, in the manufacture of linoleum.

In the cotton trade perhaps the most significant development of the period was the concentration of the industry in Glasgow and Renfrewshire, which between them came to accommodate nearly four-fifths of Scotland's cotton-mills. Few of the surviving Glasgow mills are of high architectural quality, although the Alexander Mill, Duke Street (now a hotel), designed by Charles Wilson in 1849, provides a noteworthy exception. Paisley, on the other hand, has been rather more fortunate, the Anchor and Ferguslie thread mills erected for J. and P. Coats, which with their ancillary buildings occupy an area of more than 100 acres, forming a most impressive group of mixed stone and brick construction; the finest of the Anchor Mill buildings, however, were demolished in 1973.

The woollen industry, like the linen trade, grew up largely in response to local enterprise and early manufactories tended to be small in size and widely scattered. With the introduction of finer yarns and improved manufacturing techniques during the second and third decades of the nineteenth century, however, the industry became better organized and more concentrated, although small-scale concerns like the Bridgend Mill, Islay, famous for its historic machinery, have continued to operate in more remote parts of the country up to the present day. Tweed-making was centred mainly in the Borders, the fashionable tartans trade was quickly taken up in the Forth valley, while carpets were produced at Glasgow and Kilmarnock. All these branches of the trade are today represented by buildings of interest and quality, Galashiels, Selkirk and Alva, in particular, retaining many fine groups of stone- and brick-built mills. Few firms, however, were as dedicated to the arts as Templetons of Glasgow who, in commissioning a new carpet factory in Glasgow Green in 1888, deliberately set out to create an architectural showpiece. The resulting design was not calculated to appeal to every taste, but William Leiper's Italian Gothic extravaganza of polychromatic brickwork certainly ranks as one of the most extraordinary of Glasgow's Victorian buildings.

In the case of the metallurgical and engineering industries commercial success has often proved the enemy of conservation, continuous improvements in the processes of manufacture inevitably leading to the replacement of older buildings and plant. Thus, few of the first generation of hot-blast furnaces, such as Gartsherrie and Dalmellington, can show remains as interesting and well preserved as those of their immediate predecessors (p. 132). Foundries are more numerous, however, particularly in the Falkirk and Glasgow areas, although MacFarlane's Saracen Foundry at Possilpark, famous in late Victorian times for its wide range of well designed architectural ironmongery, has recently been demolished.

93 Randolph and Elder Works, Glasgow

Glasgow, too, was at the centre of the heavy engineering industry, specializing in shipbuilding and the manufacture of locomotives. Some of

the structures erected for these purposes were fine examples of industrial architecture, one of the most notable being William Spence's immense Randolph and Elder Engineering Works, Tradeston (1858–60), whose monumental Egyptian-style façade enclosed an iron and timber framework supporting gantry-cranes and galleried floors. This was demolished in 1970, but another galleried engineering-shop (c. 1874) of similar form can still be seen at Fairfield Shipbuilding Yard, Govan, while the Vulcan Works, Paisley, illustrates an alternative method of construction involving the use of arched brickwork in place of cast-iron columns; both types were ultimately superseded by steel-framed buildings.

Among the various food-processing industries the two that produced the most distinctive architecture were brewing and distilling. Both had for long been operating largely on a domestic basis, and at least one private brew-house, dating in its present form from the early Victorian period, remains in active use at Traquair House, Peeblesshire. The larger breweries that became common after 1850 were usually of courtyard plan and incorporated their own maltings, kilns and stables, the complex being dominated by a prominent stone or brick chimney. They are situated mainly in the towns, particularly in Edinburgh, Glasgow and Alloa, whose modest-sized Thistle Brewery provides an excellent example of one of these late-Victorian enterprises. Distilleries, on the other hand, were more often located in country districts where suitable water-supplies were available, as well as barley and peat, which played an important role in the manufacture of malt whisky. With the rise of grain distilling and the introduction of blending in the second quarter of the nineteenth century the industry also began to develop in the central lowlands, but the best examples of distillery architecture are to be found in the traditional centres of Speyside and Islay.

In the field of communications the most significant development of the period was the rapid growth of the railways, which soon overtook the canal system in importance and thereafter remained the country's principal means of long-distance transport until the introduction of the internal combustion-engine. The expansion of the railway network brought great opportunities to bridge engineers and each phase of growth was marked by the construction of major works. Among the earlier bridges mention may be made of the outstanding masonry viaducts erected by John Miller on the Glasgow–Edinburgh line (Avon and Almond Viaducts, 1842) and the even more magnificent example at Ballochmyle (1846–8), which incorporates a central span of no less than 181 feet, while the Arbroath–Forfar Railway viaduct at Friockheim (c. 1840), although scarcely in the same class, is of interest on account of its curiously archaic arch-rib and slab-infill technique. Many of the later bridges and viaducts were of iron or steel construction, often utilizing masonry piers, some of the best examples of this type being in the Highlands. But masonry, brick and reinforced concrete were also employed, while at Moy, Inverness-shire, there is a remarkable five-span timber bridge of trestle-frame and multiple prop-and-

94 Connel Railway
Bridge, Argyll

beam construction reminiscent of contemporary North American practice. The best known of the later railway-bridges of the period are Sir John Wolfe Barry's Connel Bridge (1901–3), which has the second largest cantilever span in Britain, and the slightly earlier double-cantilever Forth Bridge (Sir John Fowler and Benjamin Baker, 1882–90), by common consent one of the supreme engineering achievements of its day.

The railway companies, however, had no monopoly of able engineers. Good masonry bridges of traditional type continued to be built until the end of the century, as at Glasgow (Victoria Bridge, James Walker, 1851–4), Ballater (Jenkins and Marr, 1885) and Rutherglen (Crouch and Hogg, 1896), and there are also numerous iron and steel structures, one of the finest of these being Brunel's lattice-girder bridge of 165 foot span (1857–8) which forms the approach to Balmoral Castle. Most of the surviving suspension-bridges of the period are simple footbridges, but the Portland Street Bridge, Glasgow (Alexander Kirkland and George Martin, 1851, strengthened 1871) with its elegant Greek pylons, is a large-scale work of the highest architectural quality, while two of John Justice's wrought-iron bridges (Glenisla School, 1824, and Haughs of Drimmie, c. 1830), although small in size, illustrate a method of construction in which the cantilever and suspension principles are combined in a highly original way.

Railway stations and hotels also presented favourable opportunities to designers. For the larger stations, where it was necessary to enclose and light extensive areas with the maximum degree of economy, the latest techniques of iron and glass construction were called into play and, despite recent losses, Scotland can still show interesting examples of some of the main stages of development. Haymarket Station (John Miller, 1840–2, now threatened with demolition), originally the eastern terminus of the Edinburgh–Glasgow Railway, retains an early cast-iron and timber train-shed as well as its office buildings, while in Glasgow itself, where the principal termini were remodelled during the 1870s, St Enoch (Sir John Fowler and J. F. Blair, demolished) and Queen Street Stations (James Carswell) were provided with elegant arched iron roofs, that of the former having a span of nearly 200 feet.

At the same time large numbers of urban hotels were built in a variety of styles, the railway companies themselves arguably being responsible both for the best and for the worst specimens in this field. Other byproducts of the new freedom of travel conferred by the railways were the establishment of hotels in rural areas of scenic and sporting interest, notably in the more accessible parts of the highlands, and the speedy growth in popularity of that characteristically Victorian institution the 'hydropathic'. Here, in

95 Haymarket Station, Edinburgh

disciplined relaxation, the middle and professional classes could enjoy the benefits of plain living and healthy exercise in what was to all intents and purposes an institutionalized country house, complete with well-appointed public rooms, carefully segregated service-quarters and offices, and attractively laid-out gardens, the whole being capable of accommodating upwards of 200 visitors. Although the designers of these vast establishments generally favoured the more florid styles, their products tended to be rather dull, the best features often being the elaborate sun-lounges and verandahs of glass and iron. One of the more distinguished of surviving examples, and one which still retains a good deal of its original character, is the magnificently sited French château Atholl Hydro at Pitlochry (Andrew Heiton, 1875; now the Atholl Palace Hotel), within whose lavishly equipped basement exercise-rooms the curious visitor could until recently sample Edwardian bicycling-machines and plunge-baths.

Country Houses

The early and middle decades of the Victorian age were in Scotland, as elsewhere in the British Isles, a boom period for country house building. The old landed families had never been more settled or prosperous, while to the newly rich merchant or manufacturer the purchase of an ample country estate, preferably well removed from the centre of his own commercial activity, marked an essential step in his translation to the ranks of the upper classes. For old and new families alike the urge to build or to remodel was strengthened by a growing dissatisfaction with the design and planning of the Georgian mansions in which so often they found themselves forced to live. To this was coupled an awareness that building techniques – particularly those relating to lighting and plumbing – were continually being improved, that standards of craftsmanship were uniformly high and that, given the services of a reliable contractor, a comfortable and commodious house could be erected speedily and at a moderate cost. The choice of a suitable architect was, of course, of crucial importance, and while competent practitioners could be found in most parts of the country the Scottish nobility and gentry were for more than half a century singularly fortunate in having access at 131 George Street, Edinburgh, to a firm headed successively by two of the most able exponents of country house design in Britain, William Burn and David Bryce.

Burn, the son of a prosperous Edinburgh architect-builder, had trained for some years under Robert Smirke in London before returning in 1812 to begin practice from his father's premises in Leith Walk, whence he afterwards moved to George Street. His earliest commissions were mostly for churches and public buildings, and in 1816 he was narrowly defeated in the Edinburgh University competition by William Playfair, who long remained one of his chief rivals. By the early 1820s Burn had also begun to make his mark as a designer of country houses, and his reputation grew so rapidly that he soon outshone even such established practitioners in this

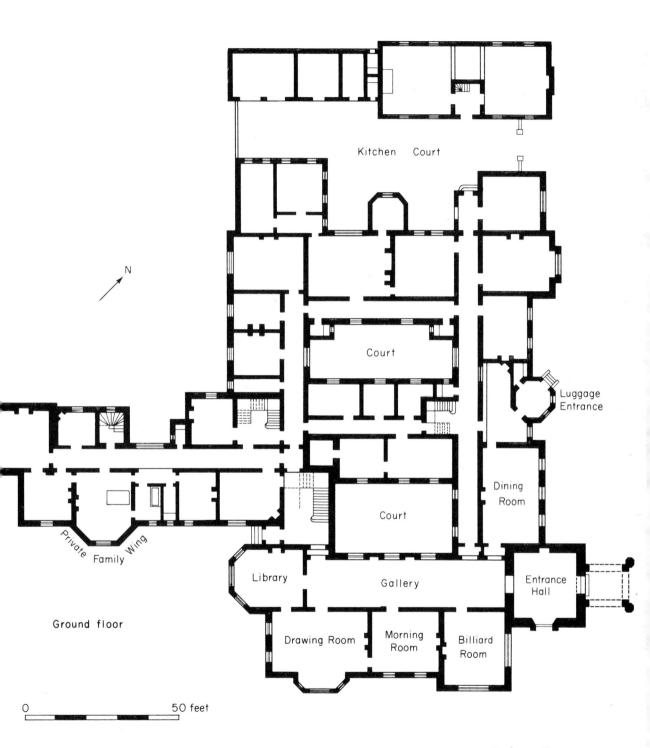

Kitchen   Court

N

Court

Luggage
Entrance

Court

Dining
Room

Private Family Wing

Library

Gallery

Entrance
Hall

Ground floor

Drawing Room

Morning
Room

Billiard
Room

0   50 feet

96 Buchanan House,
Stirlingshire: plan

field as Gillespie Graham and the Dickson brothers. Burn's practice was greatly strengthened by the appointment of David Bryce (p. 147) as an assistant in about 1825, and from then until 1844, when Burn set up office in London, the two men worked so closely together that it is often impossible to distinguish their respective contributions to a particular design. Indeed, so indispensible did Bryce become that, rather than risk losing him, Burn took him into partnership in 1841, and when the older man moved to London Bryce assumed control of the Edinburgh side of the practice, becoming fully independent in 1850 when Burn terminated the partnership following a disagreement. Burn continued to specialize in country house work and by the time of his death in 1870 had erected, remodelled or extensively altered some 200 Scottish and English mansions, while Bryce (d. 1876), although maintaining a much broader-based practice, could himself lay claim to more than 100 country house commissions, nearly all of them in Scotland.

Burn owed his success partly to certain personal qualities, in particular a willingness to take endless pains in order to meet the wishes of his clients, and partly to his abilities as a planner. Here his approach was an essentially practical one based, as one discerning contemporary observed, on 'an unswerving adherence to the common comforts of residence' and 'a strict and careful attention to the minutiae of the habits of the gentry'. Burn's achievement lay not so much in devising new forms of accommodation as in organizing the established elements of plan so as to provide the maximum degree of convenience and privacy respectively for the three main groups who made up the closely-knit community of the large Victorian country house. For the family he invariably provided a wing, or suite, of moderately-sized rooms where they could live during the winter months and retreat from guests at busy seasons of the year. Nearby would be the owner's business-room, often with its own entrance and waiting-room, while the nursery quarters, although out of earshot, would likewise be close at hand. The guests' bedrooms usually had a less favourable outlook than the family rooms, but were conveniently accessible to the main entrance and public rooms, while the various classes of indoor and outdoor servants were no less carefully marshalled in accordance with their rank, sex and sphere of occupation.

Although the majority of Burn's plans fell into one of two or three main types, they appeared in a variety of architectural styles. During the 1820s a number of his houses had reflected the fashionable Tudor mode (p. 124), but in 1822 he began to experiment with a new revival style, the 'Jacobethan', introducing shaped gables on the south front of Carstairs. Soon Burn and Bryce were producing complete houses in this idiom (Dupplin, 1828–32, demolished; Falkland, 1839–43), which remained one of the most popular in the former's repertoire.

It seems likely that Bryce also played an important part in the revival of the Scottish vernacular style, with which the firm became increasingly taken up during the 1830s. At first crowsteps, pedimented dormers and the occasional angle-turret were introduced piecemeal into houses of Tudor or Jacobean type, such as Milton Lockhart (1829, demolished) and Tynninghame (1830), but more unified and authentic compositions soon followed, often based on first-hand knowledge gained during the remodelling of sixteenth- and seventeenth-century buildings (Stenhouse, demolished; Castle Menzies; both 1836). Burn's office did not enjoy a complete monopoly of the Scottish revival movement, however, for his old competitor Playfair, although less prolific, produced several highly convincing vernacular designs. Craigcrook (1835) and Bonaly (1836) both recaptured, in their informal massing, much of the genuine flavour of the tower-house, while Barmore (now Stonefield, 1836–8), despite some rather idiosyncratic detail, successfully imitated the rambling multi-period Scots house of the pre-classical era.

But it was Bryce rather than Burn or Playfair who deservedly gained the credit for the development of the mature neo-Baronial style. The emergence of a personal manner of design, increasingly distinguishable from that of his senior partner, can be traced in a series of Burn–Bryce houses built during the 1840s and culminating in Inchdairnie (1845–7, demolished), which exhibited a number of features characteristic of Bryce's later independent work. It was at this time that the English architect and antiquary R. W. Billings was preparing the drawings for his *Baronial and Ecclesiastical Antiquities of Scotland* (1845–52), a project which had originally been promoted by Burn in London with the intention of making the book a work of joint authorship. Burn subsequently disassociated himself from the publication, however, and it was Bryce, now in charge of the Scottish office, who reaped the first fruits of the enterprise, for there is little doubt that his growing fluency in the handling of Scottish detail owed a great deal to the study of Billings's drawings.

In his working methods Bryce was content to model himself closely upon Burn, nor was he able to improve significantly upon the latter's achievements as a planner, even his characteristic garden-front terraces deriving from Burn houses of the 1820s such as Tynninghame. It was in their picturesque qualities that Bryce's houses chiefly excelled and whatever the style – and Scottish Baronial was only one of several – their boldness of massing and richness of detail gave them a panache that none could equal. The grandest and most romantic of these compositions belong to the 1850s and 1860s, when Bryce's reputation was at its height, and the houses built during this period – Panmure (Scottish Renaissance, 1852–5), Kinnaird (French Gothic, 1854), Langton (Elizabethan, 1862, demolished), Castlemilk (Scottish Baronial, 1864), Ballikinrain (Scottish Baronial, 1865) and the rest – constituted a climax in High Victorian design.

They also marked a high tide in the fortunes of the landed classes and the next generation of architects were never to enjoy quite the same opportunities for country house building in the grand manner. Many of

97 Castlemilk,
Dumfriesshire. Interior

these new men started their careers in Bryce's office, one of the most prominent of them being Charles Kinnear, who went on to establish a successful practice of his own in partnership with J. Dick Peddie. Kinnear himself seems to have handled most of the firm's country house business and was responsible for a grandiose French château design for rebuilding St Martin's Abbey (1869), which shows many of the characteristics of Bryce's own work. This never got beyond the drawing-board, however, and most of Peddie and Kinnear's houses, like Glengorm (1860) and Kinnettles (1867), were more modest in scale and Scottish Baronial in style. In general they relied very much on formulae that Bryce himself had established – the plan of Kinnettles, for example, echoes that of Balfour, Orkney (1847) – but were more stiffly composed, lacking the sparkle of their prototypes.

Another distinguished follower of Bryce was J. M. Wardrop, who practised in partnership successively with Thomas Brown and Charles Reid. Wardrop's houses are always well composed, some of the most successful of them, such as Callendar (1869–77) and Beaufort (1880–2), showing

considerable freedom in the mingling of styles. But it was R. Rowand Anderson (p. 149), Bryce's one-time partner but certainly no mere follower, who was responsible for what was probably the most eclectic as well as the most sumptuous design for a late Victorian country house in Scotland. His

98 Ballikinrain, Stirlingshire. Perspective view

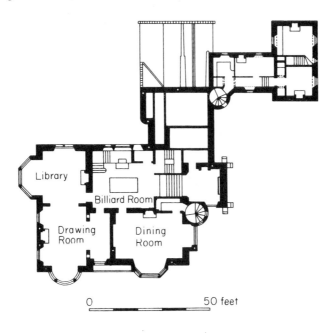

99 Kinnettles House, Angus: plan

100 Mount Stuart, Bute

client, the 3rd Marquess of Bute, was the greatest architectural patron of the day and Anderson evidently saw the commission to rebuild Mount Stuart following a fire in 1877 as a challenge to outdo William Burges's achievements at Cardiff Castle. Perhaps conceived as a romantic re-creation of the palace of some medieval prince of the church the building pays tribute to the Gothic architecture of Italy, Spain and the Low Countries, while the remarkable galleried superstructure of the four storeyed main block seems to derive from Francis I's wing at the château of Blois. The interiors are lavishly decorated with marble, stencilled paintwork and stained glass, the bronze railings of the staircase gallery being reproductions of those surrounding Charlemagne's tomb at Aachen, prepared from measurements taken by Anderson himself.

Although Scottish Baronial and some of the other established revival styles remained popular until the end of the century and beyond, the most significant developments in late Victorian country house design were initiated by a small group of architects who sought in different ways to re-interpret the domestic rather than the castellated architecture of the post-medieval period in the modern idiom. Clearly this Scottish vernacular school, with its emphasis on local building materials and traditional craftsmanship, owed a great deal to the English Arts and Crafts movement and it is not surprising to find that one of its leading exponents was C. R. Mackintosh. His interpretation was, as always, a very personal one and in their clarity of plan, directness of expression and studied control of detail Windyhill, Kilmacolm (1899–1901) and Hill House, Helensburgh (1902) reveal an entirely individual and all-embracing approach to design.

The evolution of Mackintosh's style may have been influenced by the work of the London-based Scot James MacLaren, a disciple of E. W. Godwin, whose farm buildings and cottages on the Glenlyon estate (c. 1889) anticipated several of the characteristics of Mackintosh's houses. Several of MacLaren's Perthshire commissions were completed after his death by his associates William Dunn and Robert Watson, who further developed the vernacular theme at Fortingall Inn (1891) and Glenlyon House itself (1891).

The simple and forthright character of traditional Scottish domestic architecture made a similar appeal to the young Robert Lorimer, who set up practice in Edinburgh in 1891 following brief spells in the offices of R. R. Anderson and G. F. Bodley. But while Lorimer's enthusiasm for the vernacular grew out of his early conversion to Arts and Crafts principles, his knowledge of traditional building practice was gained first hand at his

101 Hill House, Helensburgh

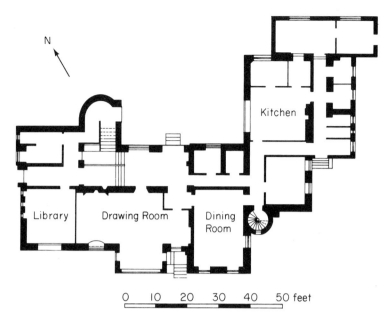

N

Kitchen

Library   Drawing Room   Dining
                              Room

0   10   20   30   40   50 feet

boyhood home of Kellie Castle and through his subsequent restorations of old buildings such as Earlshall (1891–8). In his early Scottish work, as seen at the Grange, North Berwick (1893) and in the series of small houses and cottages erected in the Edinburgh suburb of Colinton (1893–1900), he combined English and Scottish vernacular features to produce well-proportioned, often low-lying buildings with plain harled walls, mullioned windows and low-pitched roofs of tile or slate.

For the larger country houses that he built in the years before the First World War, however, (Rowallan, 1903–6; Ardkinglass, 1906–8; Formakin, 1912–4) Lorimer developed a more romantic and distinctively Scottish style which admirably reconciled the demands of contemporary planning with the employment of local materials and customary methods of construction.

103 Ardkinglas, Argyll:
plan

6
Rural Buildings

Whereas in many parts of England and Wales farmhouses of late medieval date can be found in considerable numbers, the great majority of small rural houses and cottages now standing in Scotland were erected during the course of the nineteenth century and very few indeed survive from before about 1750. This situation is the result of a countrywide revolution in standards of rural housing which began as early as the seventeenth century in some favoured lowland areas, but did not penetrate to the more remote parts of the west highlands until Victorian times. The pre-improvement dwellings of tenant farmers, tradesmen and labourers were generally mean, although standards of construction seem to have varied a good deal according both to location and to the social status of the occupant. Foreign travellers, such as John Ray and Thomas Kirke, paint a horrifying picture of housing conditions in lowland Scotland during the seventeenth century, and although their accounts may in some cases be exaggerated, the detailed and well-informed testimony of the authors of the various county volumes of the *General View of Agriculture* (c. 1790–1810) can scarcely be gainsaid, writer after writer contrasting the lamentable circumstances of the very recent past with the improvements of their own day.

The historical evidence also shows that, because they were so poorly built, these pre-improvement dwellings had a remarkably short life, total or partial reconstruction being undertaken at frequent intervals. In some areas it was customary for tenants to carry away with them the roof timbers of the house when they moved from one farm to another, a common enough occurrence at a period when farms were let without leases or upon short tenures. It is clear, therefore, that even the few remaining buildings that do, in fact, antedate the agrarian revolution are unlikely to be of great antiquity despite their often primitive aspect. Any attempt to visualize the appearance of the medieval peasant's house in Scotland must consequently be based partly upon what little evidence has so far been produced by archaeological excavation and partly upon the assumption that surviving traditional methods of construction reflect a much earlier pattern of building.

Buildings of Traditional Character
Just as medieval Scottish townsmen seem to have lived mainly in wooden houses (p. 95), so tenant farmers and rural artisans of the pre-improvement

104 Cruck-framed barn, Corrimony, Inverness-shire

era, in most parts of the country at least, appear to have dwelt in buildings of timber-framed construction. To judge from surviving examples the most common type of structure – and one that is known to have been widespread in Europe at least since late Roman times – was that in which the roof rested upon pairs of stout curved, or elbow-shaped, timbers (known generally in Scotland as 'couples', and in England as 'crucks') set at intervals along the side-walls, with their feet only a little above ground level. Robert Dinnie's account* of the methods employed in erecting houses in southern Aberdeenshire in the third quarter of the eighteenth century provides an excellent description of this form of construction. 'The couples were made with a perpendicular leg on each side of about four and a half feet in length, and were set up when the walls were built to the height of eighteen inches, with the foot of the couple resting on the inner part of the wall. The couples were placed from six to ten feet apart, and the gable tops serving the place of two, only three or four were required for a house of forty feet in length. The couples were sometimes made of whole trees, squared a little with the adze or axe, sometimes with trees cleft down the middle called half tree. In place of nails they used wooden pegs for fixing together the different parts of the couple'.

Considerable numbers of cruck-framed buildings still survive in south-west Scotland, in the central and western highlands and in the northern mainland counties, and it is probable that at one time they were to be found throughout the country, except perhaps in the outer and northern isles where suitable timber was difficult to obtain. Techniques varied a good deal from one district to another, but in comparison with English and Welsh practice standards of construction were generally poor, the cruck bays being closely spaced and the blades themselves being irregular in shape and of modest height and span. Scarfed crucks, having blades of two members scarf-jointed and pegged at wall-head level, were particularly common in the west highlands, where they continued to be built until well into the nineteenth century.

Because it could support the entire weight of a roof the cruck framework was particularly suitable for use in conjunction with non-loadbearing walls of turf, wattle or clay, but the majority of existing cruck-framed buildings have stone walls. Sometimes, as in the case of the exceptionally well-wrought and probably early barn at Corrimony, Inverness-shire, this may be the result of a later replacement of the original cladding by walls of more durable material; sometimes, as at Pitcastle (p. 175), it may be due to tradesmen's reluctance to abandon time-honoured methods of building. Other techniques of timber construction, such as box-frame, may also have been employed in some rural areas, as they certainly were in the burghs (p. 96), but no examples now appear to survive.

Turf- and wattle-walled houses were quite common throughout the

* *History of Kincardine O'Neil* (1885)

highlands as late as the eighteenth century and were probably even more widespread at an earlier period. Thus, the author of the *Statistical Account of Dornoch* (1793) mentions a part of his parish in which 'every cottage was built of feal (turf) and thatched with divot', while a year earlier Joseph Farington made a number of sketches of cruck-framed turf houses in Kincardine Moss, near Stirling, noting that they were constructed not by building up walls of cut turf, but by cutting away the surrounding peat to leave solid upstanding walls. Wattled buildings were usually termed 'creel-houses' or 'basket-houses', one particular variety being constructed with inner walls of stake-and-wattle and outer walls of turf, to which divots were pinned like slates; the thatched roof was supported by crucks. Buildings of this kind were occupied not only by tenant farmers and cottars but also by those of high social status. There is, for example, a casual reference to a 'great house constructed of wattles' at Kilpatrick, Dunbartonshire, in a document of the early thirteenth century, while prior to their extirpation in the seventeenth century the MacGregor lairds of Glenstrae possessed two

105 Wattled barn, Balmacara, Ross and Cromarty

106 Clay-walled barn, Prior's Lynn, Dumfriesshire

wattle residences, one of these being a fairly substantial building on stone foundations surrounded by a moat.

Another primitive method of building that was employed in some parts of the country involved the use of alternate courses of stone and turf, again in conjunction with a timber framework. Writing of Border cottars' houses of about the middle of the eighteenth century George Robertson described★ how a building of this type was commonly 'constructed in all its parts by the gudeman and his servants in a single day, they having previously collected the materials'.

Although building in clay was a relatively laborious process, a soundly-constructed clay-walled house afforded an exceptional degree of insulation and, so long as the external wall-surfaces were kept weatherproof by harling, enjoyed a longer life than structures of turf or unmortared stone. 'Clay biggins' are now most commonly to be found on the shores of the Solway Firth, on Coldingham Moor, Berwickshire, in the Gowrie carselands and in certain coastal areas of Morayshire and Banffshire, but

★ *Rural Recollections* (1829)

the documentary evidence reflects a much more widespread distribution in the eighteenth century. It shows, too, that at one time clay, like turf and wattle, was used to build structures of some importance, such as manses and churches.

Various techniques of construction were employed, but in most cases the clay was mixed with small stones or chopped straw, the walls often being built up in layers to prevent warping. Both loadbearing and non-loadbearing walls were used, the former normally carrying a collar-rafter roof and the latter incorporating a cruck framework. The walls were invariably raised upon stone footings and hewn stone was occasionally introduced at vulnerable points such as the jambs of doors and windows.

Stone-walled houses, too, were to be found in some parts of the country before the agrarian revolution, but the pattern of distribution is difficult to assess. So far as the southern lowlands are concerned, archaeological excavation has revealed traces of such buildings ranging in date from the thirteenth to the seventeenth century and in areas as far apart as Bute and Roxburghshire, but the evidence so far available is too scrappy to allow generalizations about their character to be made. The walls of most of these

107 Houses and outbuildings, North Uist

buildings measured between 2ft. and 3ft. in thickness and were composed of rubble masonry bonded in clay mortar, while estate papers indicate that lime-mortared buildings, too, were being erected in parts of the eastern lowlands by the seventeenth century. In the western and northern isles, however, a very different tradition seems to have prevailed from early times. Here walls were often as much as 6ft. thick, being composed of an inner and outer stone facework separated by an insulating core of turf. The Norse houses excavated at Jarlshof, in Shetland, were of this type, while Hebridean 'black houses' continued to be built in the same way until about a century ago. The roofs of black houses are usually of collar-rafter form, the rafters being set upon the inner edge of the wall, leaving the remainder of the wall-top exposed as a broad turf-covered scarcement.

The rounded corners of the Hebridean black house invited the adoption of a hipped roof, whose low rounded profile had the additional advantage of offering very little wind resistance. Turf- and wattle-walled houses also seem likely to have been hip-roofed, the cruck framework no doubt

108 Thatched farm buildings, Corr, Latheron, Caithness

incorporating an axial end-cruck of the type still found in some stone-walled buildings of cruck construction. Indeed, the gabled roof, although now almost universal except in the western isles and adjacent parts of the mainland, may in most areas be a comparatively recent phenomenon, associated with the abandonment of the open hearth in favour of the stone-built chimney (p. 176). The round-cornered Norse and early medieval houses at Jarlshof are thought to have been gable-ended, however, and the older surviving farmhouses in the northern isles are invariably gabled. In most parts of the country the roof covering itself was of thatch, but turf was also widely used, while in Orkney the lower slopes of the roof were often covered with flag-stones.

Turning next to varieties of plan-form it seems likely that the majority of farmhouses of the pre-improvement era were single-storeyed buildings of narrow linear plan, domestic quarters, byre and stable all being accommodated under a single roof. 'The byre and stable were generally under the same roof, and separated from the kitchen by a partition of osiers, wrought upon slender wooden posts, and plastered with clay', wrote the Rev. Patrick Graham* of the unimproved dwellings of Stirlingshire tenant-farmers in 1812, while a similar account of mid-eighteenth-century conditions in Ayrshire makes the point that it was customary for the cattle and the family to enter the building by a common doorway. The documentary evidence shows that the 'byre-house', or 'long house', was at one time to be found in many, if not all, parts of Scotland, and recent archaeological excavations have demonstrated that buildings of this type were erected in the northern isles as early as the 9th century and remained in use in western Perthshire until about 1800.

The dwelling accommodation of the unimproved farmhouse was commonly of 'but-and-ben' type, comprising an outer room, or kitchen, into which the outside door opened, and an inner room, which was used as a bedroom and storeroom. Some of the larger farmhouses, however, had three apartments, while others situated in less prosperous parts of the country had a single living-room only – an arrangement almost universal in the cot-houses of farm labourers and the poorer tradesmen. Internal partitions were seldom employed, rooms customarily being divided from one another by a fixed piece of furniture such as a box-bed or dresser.

A number of farmhouses contained lofts, but two-storeyed buildings were uncommon. One or two examples of early farmhouses with part upper storeys have been recorded in Orkney, however, and some well-off lowland tenants and highland tacksmen (substantial leaseholders who farmed part of their lands themselves whilst sub-letting the remainder) certainly had two-storeyed dwellings. A surviving, but ruinous example of a tacksman's house at Pitcastle, which may be as old as the seventeenth century, seems originally to have contained a large hall and small outer room on the ground-

---

General View of the Agriculture of Stirlingshire (1812)

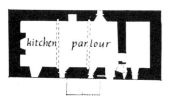

109 Pitcastle, Perthshire:
plan

floor with perhaps three bedrooms above, two approached from a forestair and one from a private staircase. The clay-bonded stone walls incorporated a cruck framework and the unglazed windows were slatted and framed; the byre and other outbuildings stood detached. The plan, which has few surviving parallels in Scotland, recalls that of certain late medieval farmhouses in England and Wales, and hints at a timber-framed building tradition based on the ground-floor hall.

The fire was usually kindled on a stone hearth in the middle of the kitchen floor, the smoke being gathered into a wide-canopied chimney constructed of wattle-and-daub or lath and plaster. An account of late eighteenth-century conditions in Peeblesshire, for example, describes a 'round-about fire side . . . that is, a circular grate placed upon the floor about the middle of the kitchen, with a frame of lath and plaster, or spars and mats, suspended over it, and reaching within about five feet of the floor, like an inverted funnel, for conveying the smoke; the whole family sitting round the fire within the circumference of the inverted funnel'. By the end of the eighteenth century, however, the central hearth was being replaced by a fireplace situated in one of the end-walls, the chimney itself being formed either as a projecting canopy or as an enclosed stone-built flue. Examples of both types

110 Long house,
Camserney, Perthshire:
plan

of construction may be seen in a byre-house at Camserney, the central hearth in this case dating from the first period of construction, when the family and cattle lodged under the same roof, and the end fireplaces (of which one has a canopied and the other a built-in flue) from a later period when the byre was converted into a separate dwelling-house.

Although a linear plan was customary, other types of layout were adopted in some areas, the most distinctive of these being that associated with the Hebridean black house. The most primitive form of black house, of which a few examples still survive on the island of Lewis, comprises an irregular cluster of three separately roofed but intercommunicating

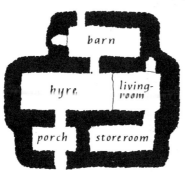

111 Black house, Lewis:
plan

buildings constructed alongside one another. The central building contains living-quarters at one end and a byre at the other, both served by the same doorway. In most occupied houses byre and living-quarters are now separated by a stone partition, but this is a comparatively recent innovation, the byre formerly having been demarcated simply by a stone kerb and timber screen. The living-quarters are usually subdivided by a light partition, the outer division comprising the kitchen and the inner the bedroom. It was formerly the custom to kindle the fire near the middle of the kitchen floor, whence the peat smoke drifted upwards through the thatch or found its way out through a smoke-hole placed a little to one side of the fire, but most houses now have end-chimneys. On one side of the central unit there is a combined stable and porch, which contains the main entrance, and on the other side a barn and perhaps also a storeroom, the former usually entered from the byre and the latter from the kitchen. The barn is provided either with a back door or a vent-hole, and there is commonly an axial arrangement of openings throughout the building to promote a through draught for winnowing. The nucleated layout often makes it impossible to light the central unit except by means of small openings contrived at the base of the thatch, and in older houses at least there is a complete absence of proper windows. The origins and antiquity of this type of plan are alike uncertain, the closest analogies being found among the traditional shieling-huts of the same area, and in the medieval and later passage-houses of Greenland and Iceland, where similar climatic conditions prevail.

The vernacular buildings of the northern isles, too, exhibit certain peculiarities of plan-form, although it is hard to say to what extent these may derive from Norse prototypes. In some of the older buildings intercommunicating apartments are ranged alongside one another, while in others ancillary chambers project at right angles to the principal range. Thus, a farm examined by Aage Roussell in 1934 at Effirth, on the mainland of Shetland, had the byre built alongside one end of the living-quarters, with the barn (perhaps in this case an addition) placed in the re-entrant angle between them; entrance was obtained through the byre. In another instance, at Conglabist, in North Ronaldsay, Orkney, living-quarters and barn were arranged linearly, while a pig-sty, stable and corn-drying kiln abutted one of the main side-walls; the byre stood detached. Few of these structures were thick-walled enough to have allowed roof drainage to have been absorbed within the thickness of the walls, as in the Hebridean black house, and although buildings were often grouped in echelon it must have been difficult to provide adequate drainage for contiguous roofs.

More typical of the traditional Shetland and Orkney farmhouse, however, is a linear arrangement in which the various units are placed end to end to form one or more ranges of intercommunicating apartments, according to the size of the farm. In its simplest form this layout corresponds very closely to that described by Dionyse Settle on the occasion of a visit to Orkney in 1577: 'Their houses are verie simply builded with pibble stone, without any chimneys, the fire being in the middest thereof. The good man, wife, children and other of the familie eate and sleepe on one side of the house and their catell on the other, very beastlie and rudely in repect of civilitie'. The dwelling-house usually contains two main apartments, namely the fire-room (or but-end) and the cellar (or ben-end), of which the former serves as a combined kitchen and living-room and the latter as the householder's bedroom. In Orkney, at any rate, these two main rooms are divided only by a dwarf-wall (known as a 'back') against which the kitchen fire is kindled, while two small additional chambers frequently project beyond the rear wall of the house, one of these being a bed-alcove and the other a storeroom, or 'ale-hurry'. In some of the larger Orkney farms the outhouses are grouped together to form a second row of buildings running alongside the main farmhouse, the intervening space between the two ranges being so narrow as to comprise a mere close rather than a courtyard. Both in Shetland and in Orkney the outbuildings frequently include a corn-drying kiln, of which two distinct types have been recorded in local use (p. 190).

Improved Farms and Cottages

It was one of the chief maxims of the agrarian reformers that well-housed tenants made better farmers than poorly housed ones. 'Nothing contributes more to the content and conveniency of a farmer, than good and well disposed buildings', wrote Dr James Anderson in 1794*, by which time a number of the more enlightened Scottish landholders had already begun to erect substantial farmhouses on their estates. In due course a similar policy of improvement was adopted with regard to the dwellings of farm servants and tradesmen, designs for all these classes of building being readily available in contemporary agricultural journals and architectural pattern-books. Improved dwellings were invariably of stone and lime construction with roofs of slate or pantile, although thatch continued to be used in some places. The model usually adopted for improved farmhouses was the small laird's house or parish manse of the eighteenth century (p. 125), that is to say a plain rectangular block of two main storeys having a symmetrical plan focused upon a central staircase. Indeed, a number of houses originally erected by bonnet lairds became farmhouses at this period, for while the agrarian revolution brought prosperity to the more progressive tenant-farmers it also led to the absorption of many small estates.

Examples of improved farmhouses can be seen throughout the country and in most cases their layout corresponds to that of the Peebleshire farms described by the Rev Charles Findlater in 1802*. 'The best farm-dwellings in Tweeddale', he wrote, 'are built in a style similar . . . to the dwelling-

*General View of the Agriculture of Aberdeenshire (1794)
*General View of the Agriculture of Peeblesshire (1802)

houses, or *manses* of the clergy. These latter are of the dimensions of from
34 to 40 feet in length, by from 19 to 22 feet in breadth, within the walls; the
door is generally in the middle of the front, whence you enter upon a very
small lobby and the staircase; on one hand is the kitchen, with a small
division, probably taken off it, for a scullery and servant's bed; on the other
hand, is generally the best room, occupying the breadth of the house for its
length. When you ascend the stair to the second storey, the space above the
kitchen may be equally divided, making two small sleeping apartments; and

112 Wester Fintray
Farm, Aberdeenshire

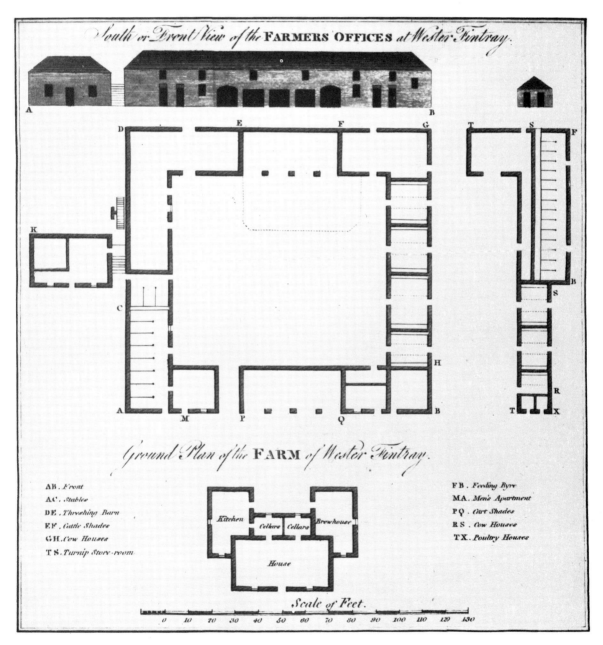

South or Front View of the FARMERS OFFICES at Wester Fintray.

Ground Plan of the FARM of Wester Fintray.

AB. Front	FB. Feeding Byre
AC. Stables	MA. Men's Apartment
DE. Threshing Barn	PQ. Cart Shades
EF. Cattle Shades	RS. Cow Houses
GH. Cow Houses	TX. Poultry Houses
TS. Turnip Store-room	

Kitchen   Cellars   Cellars   Brewhouse

House

Scale of Feet.

0   10   20   30   40   50   60   70   80   90   100   110   120   130

the space above the best room is unequally divided, affording a sort of drawing room, with a small sleeping closet. The garret space, under the roof, may be divided into a place for lumber in the one end, and the other end fitted up with a couple of beds, into what is called a *barrack* room. The farmer, having a greater number of servants than what are needed by the clergyman, is generally accommodated with a kitchen without the dwelling-house, which gives more room, though his dwelling-house is somewhat less than the manse'.

Many of these schemes of improvement made provision not only for substantial dwelling-houses, but also for the erection of farm offices upon a regular plan, a courtyard layout usually being found the most convenient. This type of arrangement had been advocated by agricultural writers, such as Lord Belhaven, as early as the end of the seventeenth century, but it was not until about the middle of the following century that the planned farm-steading began to appear in any numbers, and then mainly in southern Scotland. Among the first proprietors to adopt comprehensive programmes of improvement were the 2nd Earl of Hopetoun and the 3rd Duke of Buccleuch, while Lord Eglinton systematically rebuilt all the steadings on his Ayrshire estates soon after 1770.

As the fashion for reform spread to more remote parts of the country designs for farm-steadings and other estate works became increasingly

113 Maam Steading, Inveraray, Argyll

professional and vernacular building soon gave way to polite architecture. Thus, at Inveraray, the 5th Duke of Argyll employed Robert Mylne to erect a great court of offices in the Gothic style. Maam Steading, as it is called, was intended to be a two-storeyed courtyard building of circular plan measuring more than 200ft. in overall diameter. The southern segment, comprising a model farmhouse and stables, was never constructed, but the northern one, with its remarkable double barn and flanking cow-byres was finished in 1790 and still stands in fairly good condition. One of the most ingenious features of the design was an arrangement whereby air could be circulated through open arcades on the ground-floor, whence it rose through slatted floors to extensive corn-drying sheds on the upper storey.

Almost exactly contemporary with Maam Steading are the two rectangular courtyard-plan farms of Rotmell and Blairuachdar on the Blair Atholl estate, both probably designed by George Steuart, a local architect much patronised by the 4th Duke of Atholl. Further north many of the farms on the vast Sutherland estates were rebuilt by the Marquess of Stafford during the first two decades of the nineteenth century, most of the steadings being designed in accordance with one or two standard layouts. Two of the best examples are Cyder Hall and Inverbrora, erected in 1818 and 1820 respectively. The symmetrically planned courts of offices are very similar to one another, but the plans of the detached dwellings differ, Cyder Hall being a typical two-storeyed oblong block with a kitchen wing, and

114 Cyder Hall Farm, Sutherland: plan

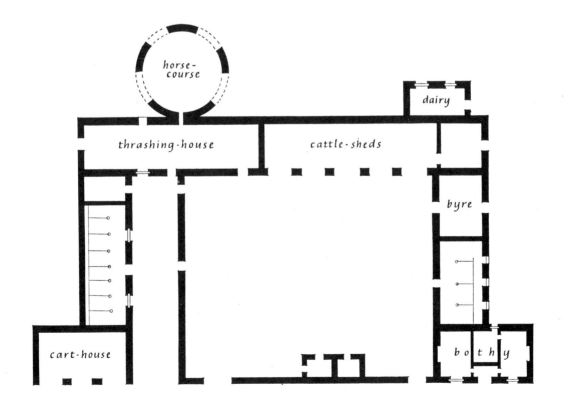

Inverbrora comprising a single main storey and a garret laid out on a miniature H-plan.

By the end of the Napoleonic Wars well-built farmhouses and steadings were to be found in most parts of the country, the most elaborate examples generally being situated in the rich arable farmlands of the eastern counties. Here the larger steadings usually incorporated arcaded cart-sheds with a granary above, cattle-shed, stable and barn as well as storerooms for root-crops and implements. Machinery for threshing and other purposes was frequently powered by horse-mills (p. 190), but in the Lothians and other areas where cheap coal was available these were already being replaced by steam-engines, whose tall brick chimneys soon came to form one of the most distinctive features of many lowland farms. Following the agricultural

depression of the post-Napoleonic era another phase of intense building activity began in about 1840 and continued for more than 30 years. During this period many steadings on the more prosperous farms were enlarged or remodelled, the new buildings often being executed in a mild version of Gothic or one of the other current revival styles.

So far as cottages were concerned, the efforts of the reformers were concentrated upon improvements in methods of construction and in standards of lighting and ventilation, rather than upon attempts to increase the size of dwellings. Substantial lime-mortared walls, slated roofs, glazed windows and built-in fireplaces and chimneys were generally considered to be the most essential items. Plans were nearly almost symmetrical, a typical layout for a two-roomed cottage comprising a room and kitchen flanking an

115 Weavers' cottages, Jericho, Angus

entrance lobby, with a mid-partition formed by box-beds; in some cases an additional bed-closet, a scullery and an outside privy were constructed at the rear. One-roomed dwellings continued to be erected for single labourers or childless couples, but the majority of cottages comprised two main rooms, either with or without a garret. Although no provision was made for housing a cow or pig, the improvers were insistent that 'no cottager should be without a garden, for it has been justly said, that a rood of land properly cultivated will half maintain a careful family'. On grounds of economy the erection of individual dwellings was avoided wherever possible, the two most popular layouts being the double cottage and the multi-unit row, and it is noticeable that these were now usually sited some little distance from the farmhouse itself.

One of the first lairds to build improved dwellings for farm labourers and tradesmen was John Cockburn of Ormiston, who began to lay out the village of Ormiston as a combined agricultural and manufacturing centre as early as 1735. Cockburn imposed stringent building regulations, even going so far as to forbid the erection of houses of less than two storeys in the main street. A few of the existing cottages in the village may belong to this initial period of expansion, while representative examples of farmworkers' dwellings of the later eighteenth century can be seen at Dunnichen, where George Dempster, one of the most eminent of the second generation of improvers, built a number of slate-roofed double cottages in 1788. Few landowners were as enlightened as these, however, and over the country as a whole progress towards better housing was slow, the main period of improvement beginning only in about the 1840s.

On many highland estates tenants were still expected to put up their own houses, but some proprietors, at least, encouraged better standards of construction by the award of money premiums. In 1832 the Highland Society of Scotland offered a premium for an essay on 'the construction and disposition of dwellings for the labouring classes, calculated to combine salubrity and convenience with economy', and afterwards sponsored publication of the prizewinning designs of the Edinburgh architect George Smith. Examples of the trim, box-like little dwellings illustrated in this and other similar pattern-books of the period may still be seen in many parts of the country, disposed either individually or in neat estate villages.

116 Improved cottage (1834)

Townships and Villages

Prior to the agrarian revolution the main unit of rural settlement was the joint-farm, held by a number of tenants in common and worked by co-operative effort. To judge from the evidence of pre-improvement estate maps the typical farm town comprised a loose cluster of buildings in which the houses of tenant farmers, interspersed with stack-yards, stock-pens and gardens, stood cheek by jowl with the cottages of tradesmen, day-labourers, ditchers and the like. In lowland districts a township of this type was often known as a 'cot-toun' and in Gaelic-speaking areas as a 'baile', a term which occurs in many highland place-names as the prefix 'bal' or 'bally'. The cultivable ground was generally divided into narrow strips, or 'rigs', each tenant being assigned a number of rigs in different parts of the farm, and in the lowlands it was customary for the well-manured rigs lying in the immediate vicinity of the township (the 'infield') to be worked more intensively than the distant 'outfield'. Throughout Scotland the practice of moving stock to upland pastures during the summer months was at one time common and although in some areas, such as the Borders, the shieling system died out during the Middle Ages it persisted in parts of the highlands until within living memory. The arrangement was designed to give the cattle the benefit of the fresh hill pastures while allowing their winter grazings to recuperate, and life in the shieling was looked forward to as a time of recreation, the women commonly employing themselves in dairying and spinning and the men engaging in various outdoor pursuits or leading lives of leisure.

So far as the lowlands are concerned virtually all traces of the traditional pattern of settlement have disappeared, the scattered farm-towns having been replaced by sizeable individual farms, and the tenants' holdings enclosed and neatly subdivided into fields; only the rigs survive as low undulations occasionally thrown into sharper relief by the slanting rays of the winter sun. In the highlands, however, the picture is rather different for in many areas almost every glen seems to harbour the ruins of an abandoned township. In the majority of cases the stone-built houses and enclosures whose remains are seen today are less than two centuries old, but the settlements themselves are often of much greater antiquity, and on some sites archaeological excavation has already begun to furnish information about earlier phases of occupation. The townships vary widely in layout. At Rosal, in Strath Naver, for example, which is known to have supported some 15 families at the time of the clearances in 1814–20, three main groups of buildings are dispersed round the periphery of the arable land, while the smaller, but better-preserved township of Auchindrain, Argyll, has a more centralised layout, the majority of the buildings clustering along the banks of a small burn that runs through the middle of the settlement. In other cases linear or rectangular clusters can be recognised, such as might have arisen as a result of early attempts at agrarian improvement. The shieling places of many of these townships can also be identified, the stone- or turf-built huts of circular or oblong plan now usually appearing as dry-stone footings or low grassy mounds.

Although quite a few burghs of barony had been successfully established as local market centres before the Act of Union, it was not until about the middle of the eighteenth century that the nucleated village began to appear in Scotland in any numbers. The main initiative in the foundation of these planned communities was again taken by private landowners, but government funds were also tapped through public bodies such as the Commissioners for Forfeited Estates and the British Fisheries Society, who were persuaded that the new villages would benefit the national economy. More than 150 villages are estimated to have been founded between 1745 and 1845, some as centres of domestic industry (usually associated with the textile trade), others as agricultural communities, and others again as fishing or harbour settlements. Although poorly represented in Fife and south-east Scotland, they occur in nearly all parts of the country, the greatest concentrations appearing in the Glasgow area, where the cotton industry provided the main stimulus, and in the north-east, where activities tended to centre upon fishing and the linen trade.

The principles adopted in village planning were similar to those that governed the layouts of contemporary towns. The two main essentials were a convenient situation with regard to water supply, building materials and communications, and a plan of regular form that could be expanded in an orderly manner if need arose, 'so that' as one improver, the Rev. Robert Rennie, wrote in 1803*, there is 'the appearance of a complete village, however small, and of a compact regular town however enlarged'. Most layouts were based either upon an axial main street or a central square or upon some combination of these two features.

Archiestown ('Archie's Town'), Morayshire, founded by Sir Archibald Grant of Monymusk in about 1760 to re-house cottars cleared from surrounding farm-towns, is a good example of a grid layout in which two main streets intersect at a central square. The village was partially destroyed by fire in 1783 and most of the existing rows of one- and two-storeyed houses, built of pink and yellow granite, evidently date from a subsequent reconstruction. Grantown-on-Spey and Fochabers have similar layouts,

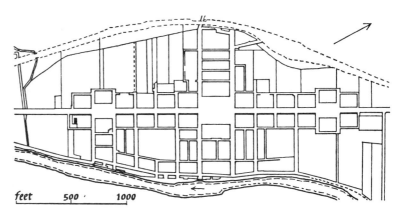

117 Newcastleton, Roxburghshire: plan

feet   500   1000

while Newcastleton, Roxburghshire (1793), an estate and handloom-weaving village established by the 3rd Duke of Buccleuch, shows a more complex variant of the same theme, the main street having a small square at each end as well as a larger one in the middle. More original was the scheme adopted by the 5th Earl of Elgin for his eponymous foundation of

*Prize Essays and Transactions of the Highland Society of Scotland II (1803)

Charlestown, Fife, a village intended to house workers engaged in the local limestone industry. The plan was that of an elongated E, building having been commenced at the middle stroke in the late 1760s and continued until the completion of the northern stroke some 50 years later.

Among the coastal villages mention may be made of the British Fisheries Society's twin foundations of Ullapool and Tobermory (1788) on the western seaboard and of the rather earlier settlement of Crovie, Banffshire, founded by the Gardens of Troup. This last is interesting on account of the absence of any formal layout, the sinuous cliff-bottom site being so narrow as to leave no space for a road of access to the houses, the majority of which present one gable-wall to the sea whilst the other confronts the cliff face. Two of the most notable early-nineteenth-century foundations were Brora (1811–13) and Helmsdale (1814), both established on the Sutherland estates of the Marquess of Stafford, the former as a coalmining and salt-producing centre and the latter as a herring-fishery port. Each was laid out on a grid plan and provided with a good harbour, that at Brora being linked to the coal-pits and salt-pans by a railway.

Mills and Kilns

The most primitive type of water-mill recorded in the British Isles, the 'horizontal mill', was nothing more than a mechanised version of the ubiquitous hand-operated rotary quern. The method of operation was extremely simple, as befitted a contrivance serving small peasant communities in which each householder was accustomed to grind sufficient meal to meet the needs of his own family. From a dam constructed across a small stream water was diverted along a lade to the mill-house, where it drove a horizontal paddle-wheel. A vertical spindle rising from the paddle-wheel passed through the lower millstone and engaged the upper one, thereby causing it to rotate. The mill-house itself, usually a small stone-built structure of subrectangular plan, comprised two chambers, the lower one housing the water-inlet and paddle-wheel, and the upper containing the working area.

Originating somewhere in the Mediterranean provinces shortly before the beginning of the Christian era the horizontal mill appears to have reached parts of northern Europe by about the 3rd century AD. None have so far been recorded in England, but they are known to have been fairly common in Ireland and in northern and western districts of Scotland, where they remained in general use until comparatively recently. Ruinous mill-houses may still be seen in considerable numbers in Shetland and the outer Hebrides, while a complete example in full working order is preserved under State care at Dounby, in Orkney.

The other main type of water-mill, incorporating a vertical wheel and geared horizontal shaft, appears to have been invented in Classical Italy and was first introduced into Britain in about the 8th century AD. The supervision and maintenance of the efficient but complex mechanism of the

118 Horizontal water-mills, Shetland

'vertical mill' was a task for a specialist, while – in western European feudal society at any rate – its high initial cost brought it under manorial control, thus giving rise to the system of 'thirlage', by which a lord's tenants were bound to have their grain ground at his mill. In medieval Scotland this type of mill was probably to be found chiefly in southern and eastern districts, and in the burghs, but existing examples most of which are of eighteenth-century or later date, are more widely distributed.

Notwithstanding the windiness of the climate, not a great many windmills seem to have been erected in Scotland – a state of affairs which is probably due to the fact that in most areas it was a fairly easy matter to harness water power. Such wind-driven corn-mills as did exist appear mostly to have been of the tower type, in which the main body of the mill is immovable and only the upper portion of the structure turns with the sails. Tower mills were invented in the Low Countries about the beginning of the seventeenth century, but most surviving Scottish examples are of rather later date.

119 Tangy Mill, Argyll

The third main source of energy used to supply rotary power for agricultural purposes was the domestic animal, usually the horse or ox. The majority of animal-powered machines incorporated some form of horizontal wheel or axle rotated about a central pivot, the equipment either being attached directly to the animal – as in the gorse-crushing mill – or worked by means of gears – as in the case of mills used to drive farm implements. In both cases the machinery was of fairly simple design such as could be operated in the open air or in outbuildings of modest size. The most interesting architectural manifestations of the horse-mill are the 'horse-gangs' or 'wheel-houses', usually single-storeyed buildings of circular or hexagonal plan, that form such a familiar feature of lowland farms.

The two main types of kiln that are likely to be met with are those constructed for corn drying and lime burning respectively. Corn-drying kilns were at one time used in many parts of Scotland, the most common variety comprising a cone-shaped chamber served by a low-level horizontal flue. They were usually built on sloping ground so that the mouth of the flue, where the fire was kindled, was easily accessible; the grain was spread

120 Wheel-house, North Bellsdyke Farm, Stirlingshire

121 Corn-drying kiln,
Kirkabist, Orkney

for drying upon a wooden rack laid across the tip of the chamber. In some
districts, however, it was customary to construct the kiln at one end of the
barn, often heating it from an internal fireplace through a short flue. In
Shetland and some other northern areas, on the other hand, smaller box-
shaped kilns were in general use, but both varieties gradually became
obsolete as more sophisticated kilns, frequently attached to corn-mills
began to appear in the late eighteenth century.

The small individual lime-kiln built to produce lime for local agricultural
or building use was similar in design to the cone-shaped corn-kiln except
that it lacked a flue. To operate the kiln layers of limestone and brushwood
or coal were thrown into the chamber from above and the fire was kindled
through an opening at the base. Lime-kilns of this type may be seen in most
parts of the country where limestone is easily obtainable, while larger
examples, some of them incorporating two or more chambers, are not
uncommon in the Lothians; most of the latter are of late-eighteenth- or
nineteenth-century date.

7
The Pattern of Building

Scottish architecture acquired its distinctive characteristics not only as a result of the historical circumstances I have tried to describe in this book, but also through response to endowed geographical factors. Of these the most fundamental was the physical contrast between the lowland and highland zones, which gave southern and eastern Scotland nearly all the advantages for human settlement, including an almost exclusive share of the prime agricultural land that was the basis of the country's wealth. Taken as a whole Scotland's geographical endowment compares unfavourably with that of many other western European countries. Small in size and remote in situation, saddled with a difficult terrain and a harsh climate, the country cannot be said to present many natural advantages for the pursuit of architecture.

One favourable circumstance is not lacking, however, namely the ready availability of good building stone, and nearly all Scottish historic buildings of any consequence are constructed of this material. Stone suitable for the erection of rubble walling can be found in most parts of the country, and the wide variety of local materials makes for strongly marked differences of colour and texture. To the observant traveller the dark greywacke of the upper Tweed valley, the sparkling granites of the north east, the grey west highland schists and the smooth regular flagstones of Caithness and Orkney compose a regional pattern no less significant than that delineated by local administrative boundaries.

Freestone capable of being dressed for ashlar walling and for ornamental work, on the other hand, is more localized in its distribution and here again the lowland counties, with their plentiful supplies of excellent sandstone, had a great advantage over highland areas. Although sandstone lacks the superb light-reflecting qualities of the finest English and French limestones, its diversity and strength of colour and its richness of texture make it an ideal material for use in a relatively sunless climate. The best known of all Scottish sandstones, the durable Carboniferous Craigleith stone used in the construction of the New Town of Edinburgh (and also widely exported) is drab-coloured and rapidly darkens in response to atmospheric pollution, and the brighter hues tend to occur in the softer Triassic and Old Red Sandstones, such as those of Dumfriesshire and East Lothian. Morayshire, Angus and Fife also contain ample deposits of first-rate sandstone, the quarries of the lower Forth valley being particularly renowned. It is known that dressed stone was shipped from Longannet and Dalgety for use near London in the later seventeenth century (p. 78), while King's College Bridge, Cambridge (1819) is built of ashlar stone from the same area.

In the west highlands the picture is a very different one for freestone is in short supply and the erection of major buildings invariably entailed the transport of building stone over considerable distances. Fortunately, the inherent difficulties of terrain were to some extent offset by the relative ease of seaborne communication, and in course of time a number of suitable quarries were located. The Loch Sween area of Knapdale contains deposits of a greenish-blue chlorite schist which when first quarried is soft and easy to carve, becoming highly resistant to weathering when exposed to air. This stone was used for the manufacture of standing crosses on Iona, some 60 miles away, as early as the 9th century, while during the later medieval period it was much in demand throughout the west highlands for the carving of monumental effigies, tomb-slabs and memorial crosses. Other local deposits of schistose rocks were also utilized, as in the erection of Inveraray Castle (p. 120), whose ashlar walls are composed of a hard blue-grey chlorite schist quarried on the shores of Loch Fyne. Sandstone, too, was available in limited quantities at Carsaig, on the Isle of Mull, and in the Ardtornish district of Morvern, and many of the medieval and later buildings of the area incorporate dressings derived from one or other of these sources, while in southern Argyll recourse was also had to the abundant New Red Sandstone beds of the Isle of Arran.

The hard granitic rocks of Aberdeenshire, although suitable enough for rubble masonry, were difficult to hew and dress with precision prior to the introduction of improved mechanical devices towards the end of the eighteenth century. Hence it was found necessary either to import sandstone dressings, as at St Nicholas's Church, Aberdeen, in the late twelfth century, or to simplify the treatment of carved details and mouldings, as in the late medieval west front of St Machar's Cathedral in the same city. Once it became possible to cut and polish granite easily, however, the advantages of its immense durability were quickly recognized and a brisk trade developed in the manufacture of paving-setts, dressed blocks, churchyard monuments and other ornamental articles, and by 1850 more than 30,000 tons of granite were being exported from Aberdeen annually. Kirkcudbrightshire also has ample supplies of granite, but this seems seldom to have been employed for building purposes prior to the eighteenth century, the earliest recorded instance of such use being in the erection of Cally House (p. 115) in the 1760s. Even when quarrying operations were greatly extended during the second quarter of the following century, comparatively little granite found its way into local buildings, the bulk of it being exported to other parts of Britain and overseas.

Scottish limestones are in general fit only for rubble walling, and what little dressed and ornamental stonework is to be found, such as the medieval coffins at the abbey of Old Deer, is of Continental or English origin. Marble, too, was imported for the construction of funerary monuments and for other decorative use. The fine recumbent effigy of King William the Lion (d. 1214) at Arbroath Abbey appears to be wrought of marble from the Frosterley quarries, Co. Durham, while during the later Middle Ages numerous slabs of dark blue Tournai marble were shipped into east coast ports as the matrices of monumental brasses of Low Countries manufacture.

But Scotland was also a producer and exporter of marble, small and remote though her quarries were. The high altar of the medieval abbey of Iona was surmounted by a slab of white marble quarried either on Iona itself or, as some would have it, on the nearby island of Skye. The Iona quarries were worked intermittently from the seventeenth century up to the time of the First World War, while during the eighteenth century attempts were also made to utilize various other marble deposits in Argyll, notably on the island of Tiree and at Ardmaddy, in Nether Lorn, whence chimney-pieces were supplied to several Scottish country houses. None of these ventures proved viable for more than short periods at a time, but at Portsoy, near Banff, the Ogilvies of Boyne managed to exploit the local deposits of variegated green and red serpentine with considerable success. It is not known when the quarries were first opened, but one of the main periods of activity seems to have been the later seventeenth and early eighteenth centuries, when items such as funerary monuments, sundials and chimney-pieces were manufactured in some quantity. The stone is said to have become fashionable in France for a brief period, and it is possible that the 'Scotch marble' chimney-pieces installed by the Duke of Lauderdale at Ham House, near Richmond, in the 1670s (p. 78) were derived from this source.

Newly-built stonework was finished off in various ways. Ashlar masonry and well-coursed rubble work were usually left exposed, the joints being carefully pointed with lime mortar. Random rubble masonry, on the other hand, was frequently harled to prevent weathering and reduce water penetration, any dressed stonework such as quoins and margins being left exposed. The lime harling was fairly coarse in texture and was either thrown directly on to the wall or applied with a small pointed trowel, both these methods of application giving a much livelier finish than modern roughcast. Whether harled or not, stone walls were often given a coat of lime wash and in some districts, such as Fife and Galloway, coloured washes were employed to great effect.

Although clay suitable for the manufacture of bricks is found in many parts of the Scottish lowlands, it was not until the later eighteenth century that brick began to be used at all widely for building purposes. This was probably due mainly to the fact that these clay-producing areas likewise contained ample supplies of good building stone. Moreover, stone-quarrying and stone-dressing were simpler processes than brick-making and better adapted to the small-scale and loosely organized operations that characterized the building trade prior to the Victorian era. At first the use of brick was largely confined to certain types of structure for which it was particularly well fitted, such as non-loadbearing partitions and the linings of ovens and ice-houses. The heat-retaining properties of brick also made it an ideal material for the construction of garden walls and it was much used for this purpose during the eighteenth century, the walls themselves often incorporating horizontal ducts for the circulation of warm air. In most cases the bricks were made on site from local materials, but in course of time many small manufactories were established, particularly in Fife and Lanarkshire, and by 1840 about 48 million bricks were being made in Scotland each year.

Stone- and brick-walled buildings, of course, also incorporated a good deal of timber and this commodity, too, was readily available in Scotland until about the end of the Middle Ages, when it began to grow scarce as a result of chronic overconsumption. The extensive primeval forests of the eastern and southern lowlands were composed mainly of oak and ash, with birch, willow and alder predominating on the higher ground, where Scots pine also flourished in certain areas. Of these, oak was by far the most valuable for building purposes, but other species were also utilized, pine being especially suitable for the production of roof-timbers. There can be little doubt that during those centuries when it was easily obtainable timber was employed even more widely than in later times when supplies had to be imported, and it seems likely that many Scottish medieval buildings, like their counterparts in England and Wales, were constructed almost wholly of this material.

Although positive evidence in the form of surviving buildings is lacking, a number of considerations support this view. Contemporary record makes it clear that prior to the seventeenth century the majority of houses in Scottish burghs were constructed mainly of timber (p. 95), while the earliest surviving rural cottages likewise reflect a longstanding tradition of timber-framed building (p. 170). It may also be significant that almost all the medieval stone castles that survive were erected by the wealthiest class of landowner, the tower-houses of the lesser lairds becoming numerous only in the sixteenth century. The virtual disappearance of Scottish medieval buildings, other than churches and major castles, is thus best explained by the assumption that they were constructed of timber and other perishable materials, and archaeological investigation has, in fact, recently begun to reveal traces of structures of this kind. To what extent these resembled early timber-framed buildings in other parts of Britain may never be fully known, but the survival of a handful of fairly elaborate late medieval timber roofs in stone churches and halls, such as that at Darnaway Castle, shows that standards of native craftsmanship in this material must not be underrated.

Finally, something may be said about roofing materials. The most widely employed material was thatch, which remained in general use in towns until the seventeenth century and in the countryside until the agrarian revolution.

Indeed, the practice of thatching still lingers today in the more remote parts of Scotland, although standards of craftsmanship are lower than they were. Methods of thatching and choice of materials varied a good deal from one part of the country to another, but straw, heather, bent grass and reed seem to have been the main substances used.

But although thatch was easy to obtain and cheap to lay, it was both perishable and inflammable, and from the medieval period onwards buildings of the better sort were increasingly covered with lead, stone or slate. Of these, lead was the most expensive and for this reason was probably used mainly for flat roofs, for which it was almost indispensable, as well as for strongly curved surfaces such as occurred in ogee-roofed steeples. Lead was mined in various places in Scotland, the principal deposits being found in the southern uplands at Leadhills and Wanlockhead. It is possible that mines in this neighbourhood were worked as early as the Middle Ages, but the main period of activity began only in the seventeenth century, one of the first recorded buildings to have been roofed with lead from Wanlockhead being Drumlanrig Castle (p. 74). At all periods local supplies were supplemented by English imports shipped via the east coast ports. In 1538, for example, lead for use at the palace of Falkland (p. 64) was imported from Hull, whither it may have been brought by river from the well-known Swaledale lead-mines.

Barrel-vaulted roofs of the type found in medieval tower-houses and collegiate churches were often covered with slabs of stone bedded directly upon the crown of the vault. In most cases, however, the load-bearing framework was of timber and it was therefore necessary to select a covering material that split easily into thin slabs of relatively little weight. Some of the Scottish flagstones, such as those of Caithness and Angus, could be utilized in this way, but the best materials were to be found among the slate beds that occur in the metamorphic rocks of the highlands and along the boundary-fault of the southern uplands. One of the earliest sources to be exploited on a regular basis was the island of Easdale in Nether Lorn, and slate slabs from this locality have been identified in several west highland castles of the fifteenth century. The industry expanded considerably during the course of the following two centuries, new quarries being opened both in the Easdale area and at Ballachulish in North Lorn. Much of this very hard dark-blue slate was shipped to Glasgow and other Clyde ports, whence it was transported throughout the southern lowlands, while during the peak years of the Victorian building boom the English and American markets, too, were supplied and annual production rose to 35 million slates. Other important slate quarries existed in the Loch Lomond area at Luss and Aberfoyle, while in the southern uplands a rather softer grey slate was obtained at Stobo and elsewhere in Tweeddale. Throughout Scotland it was customary for slates to be fixed directly to underlying sarking-boards by means of wooden pegs (later replaced by nails) rather than to be hung over battens as was usual in England.

In parts of eastern Scotland, particularly Fife and the Lothians, thatch gave way during the seventeenth and eighteenth centuries not to slate but to red pantile. Pantiles are generally supposed to have been introduced into Scotland as ballast for incoming boats from the Low Countries and this may well be true. But tiled roofs of one sort or another were not unknown in Scotland in medieval times, and licence was sought for the manufacture of 'good and sufficient tyill for building and sclaitting of houssis' as early as 1611. It seems likely, therefore, that, as in England, imports were gradually supplanted by local products, while during the eighteenth century tiles were often manufactured jointly with bricks, which were made from similar materials.

Further Reading

In compiling the following list the main emphasis has been placed upon books of recent date that are fairly easy to obtain. Much valuable material is also published in the form of articles in journals and periodicals and these are listed annually in *The Scottish Historical Review* and in *Discovery and Excavation, Scotland* (published by the Scottish Regional Group of the Council of British Archaeology).

Apted M R *The Painted Ceilings of Scotland* (1966).

Beard G *Decorative Plasterwork in Great Britain* (1975).

Beresford M and Hurst J G *Deserted Medieval Villages* (1971).

Boucher Cyril T G *John Rennie 1761–1821* (1963).

Butt John *The Industrial Archaeology of Scotland* (1967).

(Cant R G) *Old Moray* (1948); *Central and North Fife* (1965); *St Andrews. The City and its Buildings* (1967).

Cant R G and Lindsay Ian G *Old Glasgow* (1947); *Old Stirling* (1948).

(Cant R G and Lindsay Ian G) *Old Elgin* (1954).

Colvin H M *A Biographical Dictionary of English Architects (1660–1840)* (1954).

Crossland J Brian *Victorian Edinburgh* (1966).

Cruden Stewart *Scottish Abbeys* (1960); *The Scottish Castle* (1963).

Donnachie Ian *The Industrial Archaeology of Galloway* (1971).

Donnachie Ian and Macleod Innes *Old Galloway* (1974).

Drummond A I R *Old Clackmannanshire* (1953).

(Dunbar J G) *Sir William Bruce* (1970) (Exhibition Catalogue).

Edinburgh Architectural Association *Edinburgh, An Architectural Guide* (1964).

Fawcett Jane *Seven Victorian Architects* (1976). (Contains chapter on William Burn by David M Walker)

Fenton A *Scottish Country Life* (1976).

Fenwick Hubert *Scotland's Historic Buildings* (1974).

Fiddes Valerie and Rowan Alistair *David Bryce 1803–1876* (1976) (Exhibition Catalogue).

Fleming John *Scottish Country Houses and Gardens open to the Public* (1954); *Robert Adam and his Circle* (1962).

Forman Sheila *Scottish Country Houses & Castles* (1967).

Gauldie Enid *Cruel Habitations. A History of Working-Class Housing 1780–1918* (1974).

Girouard Mark *The Victorian Country House* (1971).

Gomme Andor and Walker David *Architecture of Glasgow* (1968).

Grant D *Old Thurso* (1966).

Grant I F *Highland Folk Ways* (1961).

Hall Robert de Zouche *A Bibliography on Vernacular Architecture* (1972).

Hannan Thomas *Famous Scottish Houses* (1928).

Hay George *The Architecture of Scottish Post-Reformation Churches* (1957); *Architecture of Scotland* (1969).

Hill Oliver *Scottish Castles of the sixteenth and seventeenth centuries* (1953).

Hitchcock Henry-Russell *Early Victorian Architecture in Britain* (1954).

Howarth Thomas *Charles Rennie Mackintosh and the Modern Movement* (1952).

Hume John R *The Industrial Archaeology of Glasgow* (1974); *The Industrial Archaeology of Scotland* (1976–   ).

Hussey C *The Work of Sir Robert Lorimer* (1931).

Knoop D and Jones Q P *The Scottish Mason and The Mason Word* (1939).

Lindsay Ian G *Old Edinburgh* (1947); *The Scottish Parish Kirk* (1960); *Georgian Edinburgh* (1973).

Lindsay Ian G and Cosh Mary *Inveraray and the Dukes of Argyll* (1973).

Lindsay Jean *The Canals of Scotland* (1968).

Macaulay James *The Gothic Revival 1745–1845* (1975).

MacGibbon D and Ross T *The Castellated and Domestic Architecture of Scotland* (1887–92); *The Ecclesiastical Architecture of Scotland* (1896–7).

Mackenzie W Mackay *The Medieval Castle in Scotland* (1927).

Macleod Robert *Charles Rennie Mackintosh* (1968).

McAra Duncan *Sir James Gowans, Romantic Rationalist* (1975).

McWilliam Colin *Scottish Townscape* (1975).

Millman R N *The Making of the Scottish Landscape* (1975).

Morton R S *Traditional Farm Architecture in Scotland* (1976).

Petzsch H *Architecture in Scotland* (1971).

Pratt E A *Scottish Canals and Waterways* (1922).

Pride Glen *Glossary of Scottish Building* (1975).

Renn D F *Norman Castles in Britain* (1968).

Richardson A E *Robert Mylne, Architect and Engineer, 1733 to 1811* (1955).

Richardson James S *The Medieval Stone Carver in Scotland* (1964).

Rolt L T C *Thomas Telford* (1958).

Roussell Aage *Norse Building Customs in the Scottish Isles* (1934).

Royal Commission on Ancient and Historical Monuments (Scotland) County *Inventories* (1909–   ).

Salmond J B *Wade in Scotland* (1938).

Scott-Moncrieff G *The Stones of Scotland* (1938).

Service Alastair *Edwardian Architecture and its Origins* (1975).

Simpson W Douglas *Scottish Castles* (1959); *The Ancient Stones of Scotland* (1965).

(Simpson W Douglas) *A Tribute – to the Memory of William Kelly* (1949).

Sinclair Colin *The Thatched Houses of the Old Highlands* (1953).

Smiles Samuel *Lives of the Engineers* (1861).

Summerson John *Architecture in Britain 1530–1830* (5th edition 1969).

Taylor William *The Military Roads in Scotland* (1976).

Thomas Charles *The Early Christian Archaeology of North Britain* (1971).

Tranter N *The Fortified House in Scotland* (1962–70).

Walker David M *Architects and Architecture in Dundee 1770–1914* (1955).

Young Andrew McLaren and Doak A M *Glasgow at a Glance* (1965).

Youngson A J *The Making of Classical Edinburgh 1750–1840* (1966).

Index

Place-names are listed under historic counties, not under current regions and districts. The numerals in bold type refer to the figure numbers of the illustrations.